God, Prayer and Spirituality

A Collection of Sermons

Rabbi Stuart Weinblatt

Jay Street Publishers, New York, NY 10023

ISBN 1-889534-17-X

Jay Street Publishers, New York, NY 10023

The publication of this book is made possible by a generous contribution by Patti and Allan Bergenfield in loving memory of Sue Gingold.

CONTENTS

Introduction

The sermon is a unique form of communication. It is more than just communication. It is a means of conveying a message.

The challenge is to address issues facing us in the context of Judaism or, conversely, to show how the ancient teachings of Judaism can influence and play a role in our lives. The sermon bridges these worlds and offers the chance to teach how the two interact and how our tradition can help us deal with life. This is why I strive to make my sermons timely and relevant by drawing upon the wellspring of our tradition and heritage as well as what is happening in contemporary culture.

The process of determining the subject and then of composing the sermon is like creating a piece of art. Structure and form must merge to present the content in a way that has meaning and will hopefully have an impact upon those who hear it.

With the advent of the internet, written material can take on a life of its own. Spoken words originally heard can be transcribed and circulated rapidly around the globe and beyond one's community. But there still is nothing like a book to preserve and capture one's writings.

In this first of what I hope will be several volumes, I have collected sermons I have delivered over the years that address the subject of the title: ***"God, Prayer and Spirituality."*** Having founded and built a congregation from scratch in 1988, the sermons I gave about the significance of the synagogue and its role as a progenitor of Judaism are also included. It is my hope to share in future volumes my sermons on the subject of Jewish peoplehood, the centrality of Israel, Jewish ethics and Judaism's values and insights for living.

I am indebted to those who helped to make this publication possible.

I am extremely grateful to Patti and Allan Bergenfield. Without their generous support and encouragement this project would never have become a reality. It is an honor to pay tribute to the memory of Patti's mother, Sue Gingold, with the publication of this collection.

I appreciate B'nai Tzedek and its members, my congregation, which has supported, encouraged and challenged me to continue to grow. I think lovingly of my parents who took pride in my accomplishments.

Most of all, I thank my family: my wife and companion, Symcha, who provides inspiration, counsel and advice and who has taught me so much. I also thank my loving children, Ezra, Margalit, Micha and Noam, who constantly amaze me anew with their infinite qualities and attributes, and who strive to live their lives in accordance with the teachings of our faith.

May 2008

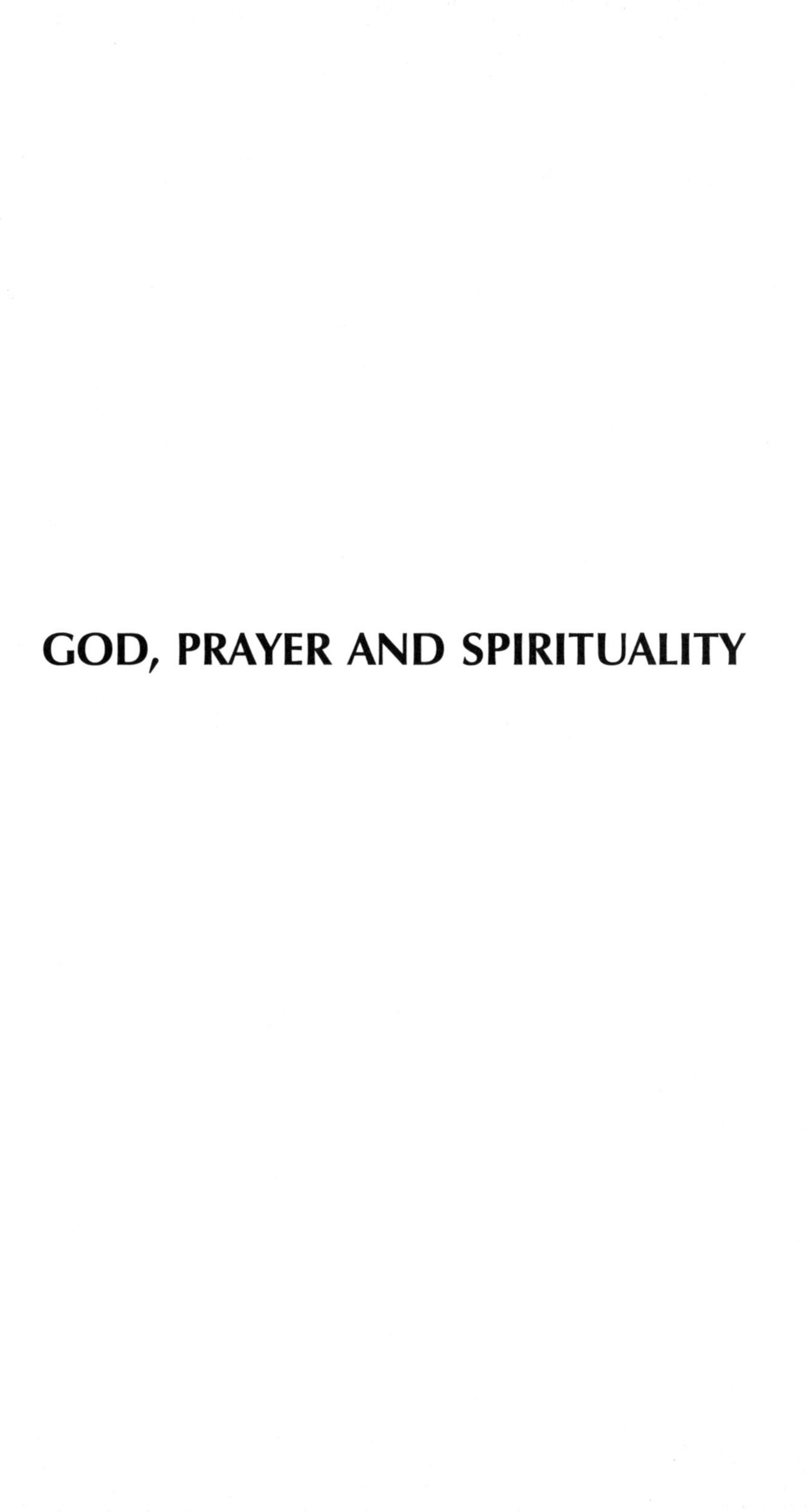

GOD, PRAYER AND SPIRITUALITY

What I Love About Being Jewish

From time to time, and especially at this time of year, we may wonder why we are here, what life is about and why life is as it is. Religion offers a means of making sense of these existential questions. It provides a framework to help understand things that happen to us as well as comprehend the events and catastrophes that occur in our world.

We may ponder our fate and existence and ask: Why is our lot what it is? Is it predetermined, or do we have any influence over the outcome? If the nature of our fate is predetermined, then who makes that determination? And, furthermore, when, how, and on what basis is it decreed? If we are masters of our fate, then on what basis should we decide how to act? Is this life all there is? If there is an afterlife, what is it like? What are the criteria for admittance? If we have no afterlife and this is the end of our existence, then what is the point to having lived? And if there is a purpose or meaning to life, then what is the value of living with all the difficulty it entails?

Reflection on these issues may lead us to ask other questions, such as: What should be our goals in life? Should we live just to enjoy material pleasures, or is there something more important in life? One of the biggest, unanswerable mysteries also commands our attention and attracts our speculation: what happens after we die?

The issues are not new and have, in fact, perplexed the human race since the beginning of time. These ultimate issues have been raised by each generation. Every religion, as well as secular philosophies which are not religions, attempt to respond to these questions. Ancient religions offered answers reflecting world views immersed in superstitious beliefs and which may seem primitive and unsophisticated by modern standards.

Judaism has brought unique responses to these questions. Despite being such an ancient tradition, it is amazingly modern in its outlook. We derive comfort from combing our tradition and reading venerated texts and sources and thereby discovering that our sages grappled with so many of these same questions which plague and baffle us today. Even more amazing and refreshing is seeing the doubts and skepticism evident in their responses.

Part of the attraction to Judaism, for me, is intellectually motivated. I am a Jew, not so much because of the answers given, but because of the questions it asks. I love the fact that our sages did not bequeath to us one packaged "take-it-or-leave-it," "one-answer-fits-all" response. Unlike other religions which present simplistic, clear-cut answers to these questions, Judaism often does not offer uniform responses. Rather, it offers a plethora of profound possibilities. While offering a perspective and means of understanding our world, sometimes the responses may even be in conflict and in tension with one another. At other times, our sages confess their inability to comprehend that which is beyond them – thus encouraging us to continue to ask the questions and to continue the quest for the answers.

I love Judaism and love being a Jew, because I believe in looking at the world and exploring questions about life and what happens to human beings from a Jewish perspective. I appreciate what our religion teaches us. Judaism is unusual among world religions, because it calls upon us to study the various responses given by our sages and then to use our intellect to decide which approach to accept.

I am drawn to Judaism, because, in addition to how it challenges me spiritually and intellectually, it moves and touches my soul in unimaginable ways. I am constantly inspired to be a part of this remarkable people. To be a Jew is to be part of a people, a culture, a civilization. It is a way of life and of living. Judaism's values are all so life-affirming, reasonable, sensible and intelligent. Our customs, rituals and traditions combine with a sense of being a people who endeavor to live morally and who value the need to work for *tikun olam,* the obligation to improve the world and to seek to create a just society. We are a small people, who, beyond our numbers, have had a profound and disproportionate impact on the world.

We are a people who have walked in history for 3,500 years, who adapt and preserve, and who strive to bring the message of God to everyday life without imposing or forcing it on others against their will.

All of this is what I find so inspiring, uplifting, exhilarating and fulfilling about being a Jew. This people, this tradition, this heritage, its teachings, aspirations, yearnings and message are what give meaning, purpose, joy and fulfillment to my life and to me.

Erev Rosh Hashana
September 22, 2006

God

People have called Jews a God-intoxicated people, for the concept of God is at the heart of the Jewish message. Jewish philosophers recognize that a belief in God is either based upon personal faith motivated by personal experience or occurs because one inherits the concept from one's ancestors. This is why the Amidah begins with the salutation *"Eloheinu, v'elohei avoteinu:* Our God and God of our ancestors," so as to include both types of believers.

Or, as a little girl responded when asked why she believed in God, "I don't know. I guess it just runs in my family."

Considering how important God is to the Jewish experience, it is surprising that proving the existence of God occupies such a small portion of our classical writings. The Torah itself opens with the words, "In the beginning God. . ." It does not tell us of God's origins or lineage. The Torah assumes from the outset the existence of a God and that this God is, in Aristotelian terms, the "Prime Mover" behind the creation of the Universe.

Yet, as Rabbi Neil Gilman points out in his book, *Sacred Fragments,* God has many faces or aspects and is more than the Creator of the world. Our God is multi-dimensional. The God of Hanukah is different than the God of Rosh Hashana, which is different from the God of Passover. Part of the thrill of living a life as a committed Jew all year round is to experience the many different facets of the Almighty. One of the problems with having only partial or occasional limited exposure to the Jewish calendar and liturgy is that one comes away with an incomplete picture of our people's perception of Providence.

Judaism's concept of God is not monolithic. The *midrash* pointedly notes that although God revealed the Torah to 600,000 Jews all at once, He addressed them in the singular form. *"Anochi Adonai Elocheca: I* am the Lord your God." The rabbis dared to teach the radical notion that each individual perceives God in a unique way. God is not monochromatic.

According to Rabbi Levi in the Talmud, "God appeared to Israel in infinite images reflecting the appearance of each individual, and all felt personally addressed." Many centuries later Rabbi Nahman of Bratslav agreed that individuals experience God through the "gates" of their own hearts.

The monotheism introduced by the Patriarchs to the world was not innovative because it reduced the number of gods one worshipped. Rather, it was revolutionary because it conveived of God as above nature, not in nature. Monotheism departed from paganism and polytheism by depicting a God as caring about how human beings act. The prophets were not just monotheists, they were *ethical* monotheists. Affirmation of one God is not a mathematical statement, but a moral one.

Our tradition also teaches that finite minds cannot expect to fully comprehend the infinite God. The medieval Jewish philosopher, Maimonides, put it this way, *"Lu yadativ, hayitiv:* If I knew God, I would be God."

Judaism also asserts that room exists for doubt, for questioning and for challenging God over the suffering and injustices in our world. These objections are traditional responses to the problems of living. There are many Hasidic stories of Rabbi Levi Itzhak of

Berditchev and others pointing an accusing finger at God, especially at this time of year.

There is a relevant and wonderful joke about a very devout and religious man who was in the middle of the sea on a boat which suddenly started to sink. While all the other passengers frantically rushed to get life preservers and ran to the life boats, he did nothing.

As things got worse, he climbed atop the sinking ship and patiently waited for God to save him. A rescue boat came and the coast guard called for the man to get in. Stubbornly he explained, "That's okay," thinking to himself, I am a religious man. I know God will save me.

After the boat left and as the water continued to rise, almost consuming him, a helicopter came by and lowered a rope for him. Once again he refused help, maintaining that it wasn't necessary since God would be his salvation. So he waited in the belief that God would come and miraculously save him from impending disaster.

Shortly thereafter, the water level continued to rise and the man drowned. When he got to heaven, he expressed his shock. Angrily he confronted God, "All my life I have been faithful and worshipped you. I have followed your teachings. And now you let me down. Why didn't you come to save me?"

God simply responded, "What are you talking about? Who do you think sent you the boat and helicopter?!"

The story reminds us that at the heart of our Jewish belief in God is the notion that we have a personal relationship with Him.

But we cannot manipulate or control God. Rather, Judaism asserts the unique idea that God is dependent upon us both for His presence and to bring about His influence in the world. The source of goodness that is God manifests itself in the acts of kindness we perform towards others. The love which God has implanted within His creatures is realized when we express love for another creature.

That God is dependent on us is noted in a verse in the Book of Psalms, "Man abides in the Shadow of the Almighty." One rabbinic interpretation asserts that this means that God exists as a human shadow. A human being stooping low diminishes God, but a person standing upright lifts God on high. It is up to us to decide whether or not we exalt God and allow the spirit of the divine to enter our lives and influence us or if we reduce and lessen this essence.

We are, in the words of the Talmud, *"shituf poalo:* God's partners in creation." Created in the image of God, we realize and fulfill that calling when we work for *tikun olam,* making the world a better place. When we feed the sick, clothe the naked, raise up the lowly – when we perform *mitzvot,* which God demands of us – we are living up to God's finest expectations. The Talmud asserts that when we do these simple acts, heaven and earth touch.

Throughout the centuries our faith has been more concerned with helping us to live our lives understanding what it is that God asks of us, than in trying to get God to do what we ask of Him. The message of this morning's *haftarah* from the prophet Isaiah is that we cannot go to synagogue regularly, then do something unethical and expect God to be pleased. Reciting prayers should help us learn what it is that God demands of us, which is meant to help us become better people.

Many contradictory images of God co-exist in our heritage. God is transcendent and beyond description, yet God is a personal God, interested in each individual. God's greatness is not an impediment to His nearness. In fact the nearness of God is the source of His greatness.

As the Talmud puts it, "God is so great and vast, yet he can hear the faintest whisper uttered behind a pillar in any synagogue."

Our prayers at this season remind us that God remembers all our deeds, things which we have long forgotten. This may be a difficult concept for modern rational people to fathom. Yet, it is also one of Judaism's most important ideas. We may not believe that God intervenes in our world to direct the course of events, but we should still live our lives with the knowledge that what we do matters to God.

This concept of the all-seeing God, according to Judaism, is the source of morality in our world. Subjective morality – without any absolutes and in which each person or society determines what is right and wrong – is risky. The famous quote from Doestoevsky is appropriate: "If there is no God, everything is permitted."

Rather than focus on what God is like and whether or not God exists or does not exist, we should focus on what kind of people the God of our religion wants us to become. Rabbi Harold Kusner in his book, *Who Needs God,* wrote: "A God who exists, but does not make a difference in the way you live might as well not exist. . . The issue is not what God is like. The issue is what kind of people we become when we attach ourselves to God."

What is critical about our relationship with God, when praying out loud, is that God hears our prayer and that our hearing it helps us to learn what it is that God hopes we will become. Not that God grants all our wishes. After all, God is not Santa Claus.

In *The Healer of Shattered Hearts* David Wolpe reminds us that Jewish tradition has always taught that God shares our pain and sorrow, that He grieves with us, and that He is with us when we suffer. A caring God is not indifferent to the agony of His creation. Rabbi Wolpe put it this way, based upon a story in which Reb Levi Yitzhak of Berditchev said, "Dear God, I care not why I suffer. I wish only to know that I suffer for your sake."

We might adapt his prayer and put it in modern terminology, "Dear God, I care not so much why I suffer. I wish only to know that you share my pain."

The journey towards God is not easy, for the target is often beyond our grasp and difficult to conceive of or perceive. But the effort to experience the Divine is inherently worthwhile. Our heritage and tradition serve as a guide for the search for God. The quest itself is what gives us sustenance and strength. Isaiah said, "And those that yearn for God shall find renewed strength. They shall spread out their wings like eagles."

I read that when Rabbi Levi Kelman was a child, he asked his father the following question: "If God was invisible, could God see Himself?"

His father, Rabbi Wolfe Kelman, could not answer at first. But then several days later he came and told his son at bedtime, "When you see yourself, where do you look?" The little boy answered, "In a mirror."

The father said to his son, "Well, when God wants to see Himself, He looks at you to see if He can see Himself in the best of what you do."

In the year to come may we live our lives so that God will see Himself in each and every one of us and in what we do.

Yom Kippur
5752/1991

Prayer

Our Torah portion on Yom Kippur morning describes the ancient ritual performed in the days of the Temple, wherein the Kohen Gadol, the High Priest, would send away the goat that symbolically bore the people's sins. Later this afternoon we will once again pay tribute to the dramatic Temple ritual with the hazzan's reenactment of the early Temple service during our *Avodah* service.

At one time prayer was the exclusive purview of the priests. But in the thrust for democratization and inclusiveness that followed the destruction of the Temple, prayer came to take the place of sacrifice. The Talmud quoted Rabbi Joshua as lamenting the destruction of the Temple and Rabbi Yohanan reassuring him saying, "Do not grieve. There are other ways to make atonement even though the Temple is destroyed." The rabbis taught that our prayers and deeds of loving kindness would take the place of sacrifice.

Researchers and sociologists tell us that there is a spiritual hunger in America. Dr. Wade Clark Roof in his book, *A Generation of Seekers,* documents the emptiness many experience in their lives. He writes, "People are looking for a place where they feel comfortable" and look to fill their spiritual needs in a variety of outlets. While Jews are well represented among those pursuing spirituality, unfortunately for too many Jews, the last place they think to look is the synagogue and traditional prayer. A recent study by Andrew Greeley reveals that 78% of all Americans pray at least once a week and that

57% report praying once a day. But this is not the case in our synagogue or the Jewish community as a whole.

We, the people who developed and spread the concept of monotheism to the world, who are heirs to an eternal covenant with the Master of the Universe, attend services in smaller numbers than members of other religious groups, according to numerous surveys.

Going back a couple of centuries Rabbi Nahman of Bratzlav was always tolerant of his fellow Jews and their resistance to praying in synagogue. He refused to see anything but the virtues of his fellow Jews. One day as he was walking through the town shortly after morning prayers, he saw a member of his congregation changing the wheel of his carriage. This Jew did not take time to stop and come to morning *minyan* to recite his prayers, but mumbled them somewhat hurriedly while changing the wheel. But rather than criticize him or condemn him for misplaced priorities or a lack of *kavannah,* Rabbi Nahman praised the man. He lifted his eyes and said to God, "Look at how wonderful a people you have. Even while fixing a wheel, your people take time out to say prayers of praise to you." He used to comment in a similar vein when people would talk during services: "How wonderful are your people, Oh Lord. Even while they are talking, they still take time to pray to You."

We are not the first to find it difficult to pray. The words may get in the way because they are in a foreign language. Even when the words are in English, they may not be part of our regular lexicon or thought. The liturgy may be unfamiliar to those without exposure to it or for those who did not grow up in a traditional synagogue. But if these are the only problems distancing us from prayer, we can overcome them by education, exposure and practice. There are other reasons we feel alienated.

Perhaps we are so rational that we cannot fathom how prayer can do anything. We rarely place ourselves in a dependent relationship or in a position where we would have to confront or recognize our limitations– and honest prayer may entail this. Used to the rapidly moving barrage of visual images constantly placed before our eyes on various screens, prayer is a different kind of experience. We may be uncomfortable in such a setting and may find services not to be meaningful or even boring. In a utilitarian society we question what it can do for us.

In an article entitled, *Why You Can't Pray and What You Can Do About It,* Jewish Theological Seminary Professor of Theology and Liturgy Dr. Neil Gillman, writes that, "Nothing in religious living is more difficult to achieve than a moment of genuine prayer. Don't suppose that only you have this problem." He asserts that even rabbis may have problems in this area, for "It is relatively easy to be a moral person or to devote a few moments of every day to the study of Torah. . .Prayer, however, is not a matter of will alone. It requires a coming together of feeling, thinking and discipline and even if you want to accomplish this, there is no guarantee that you will succeed."

Afraid of failure, we do not even try. Some of us find it difficult to reach beyond our own inner selves and recognize a force beyond us or a power within us. I have always felt that prayer entails reaching in two directions – to the power in the universe which is transcendent and often seems to be beyond my reach and also to the immanent untapped source of energy within my soul.

All too often I, like you, find that rote recitation of the ritual and traditional prayers may inhibit serving the Divine. This is why it helps to ponder, reflect upon and understand the words of our prayers. To be truly carried and lifted to spiritual heights we must also add ideas from our own thoughts and life experiences to the words on the pages of our prayer book. Our sages recognized this, for the Talmud tells us, "If one has not added his own words to the prayers, it is as if he has not prayed." But the truth is that too many traditional and conservative synagogues neglect this teaching and don't give us the opportunity for individual prayer. So when I pray, I add my own thoughts, usually at the end of the *Amidah* and encourage you to do so as well. Sometimes I have said during services out loud or to myself, "Don't forget to pray while praying."

Yet our tradition counsels that we cannot depend solely upon our own inner feelings. The traditional prayers of the *siddur* link us to our past and anchor us in Jewish thought and milieu. They help to provide a framework and means of approaching God which places us within the continuum of previous generations as well as tying us to other Jews around the world. Many people have had the experience of finding themselves in a different city or country and being overcome by a sense of oneness with their fellow Jews, because they feel united by the prayers they have in common. This has happened to me in synagogues in Russia and Israel and outside the crematoria of Matthausen as well as in airport waiting lounges with rabbinic colleagues on our way to visit Jewish communities in Europe. I felt the connection with my fellow Jews and was inspired in those places and on those occasions partly because I was not a stranger to the regular service.

When we approach God in prayer, we clearly confront a power greater than us. We may feel overwhelmed and intimidated by the images evoked by such words as the "King of the Universe" when we pray.

I once saw a cartoon of a mother listening to her child praying to God. She interrupted him to tell him he could just *say* his prayers. It wasn't necessary to give God his social security number.

Rabbi Harold Shulweiss of California has written, "Prayer is difficult. But that difficulty is not with grasping understanding of the Other." He contends prayer is difficult because we are uncomfortable confronting ourselves. The Hebrew word for prayer, *l'hitpallel,* is a reflexive verb implying that in our tradition prayer involves self judgment. So we in our discomfort make excuses and say we do not have the time to come to services once a week or that we do not expect to get anything out of the experience.

But we may have the wrong expectations of what prayer can do. Another cartoon I saw was one in which a child told his parents he didn't need to say his prayers that night. "Why not?" they asked him. He answered that he didn't need anything that night. Prayer is much more than just asking for what we want or think we need. It allows us to confront our fears and ourselves. It's not that God doesn't hear or answer our prayers. It's just that sometimes the answer is no.

We expect that prayer will change the world. It may, but it probably won't. Prayer, however, is much more likely to help transform us. Saying a prayer will not mend a broken bridge, but it may help to heal a broken heart. Praying may help us to find the inner strength to deal with the vicissitudes of life.

Our tradition cautions us about the limits of prayer. A fascinating passage in the Talmud says that King Hezekiah received praise for hiding the *Book of Healing* during his reign. The great physician and philosopher, Maimonides, explained this passage. The people were criticized for relying too much on the book and miracles and not on physicians. Judaism does not want us to view prayer as a panacea, but as part of what we do. The Talmud tells us to pray as if everything depends on God, but to act as if everything depends on us.

Thinking about the importance of prayer reminds me of the joke about the Jew and the Christian Scientist with similar problems who were sharing a hospital room. Whenever the doctor got near the gentile, the patient would grimace and scream in agony. Yet the Jewish patient experienced no pain. Finally one day the Christian Scientist could not take it any longer. He asked his roommate how it was that he felt nothing while he, who was trained to suppress feelings of pain and rely on God, couldn't stand it when the doctor touched his leg. The Jewish patient turned to his friend and said, "What makes you think I show him the bad leg?!"

The medieval Jewish philosopher, Joseph Albo, advised us not to believe that our uttering of words will somehow change the destiny and cosmos of the universe. Who are we, he asked, to dictate to God what to do? How can we know what is best for us or the world? Albo counseled instead that the best prayer is to ask God to do what is best.

Author Julius Lester writes, "The words of Jewish prayer are an exalted language, used to address God alone (which) identifies and reminds us of what is important. . .enabling the soul to be articulate in the face of its Creator. The language of prayer enables us to say 'Thank you' for this precious life You have given us." Dr. Arthur Green states that, "Prayer doesn't work. You work. Prayer is the singing out and longing of one's heart to the one who made the world." Neil Gillman likens creating a prayer to "a subtle and complex work of art."

Jewish prayer is disciplined, with fixed times and

rules and regulations. But what we learn from our tradition is that we should not feel restricted or encumbered by the words. A wonderful story in the *midrash* says that the birds complained to God that they were weighted down by the burden of the cumbersome wings He had given them. God responded, "Silly birds, don't you realize that the wings I gave you were meant to make you free and to carry you upwards."

The rabbis said this was analogous to our attitude about the *mitzvot.* I would contend that the message also applies to our *tefillot,* our prayers. They are meant to carry us heavenward towards God.

Finally, my friends, of all the reasons Jews come to the synagogue to pray, perhaps the most important is not that this is where we find God or inner peace, but that this is where we find our fellow Jews. It is no coincidence that Jewish prayers are written in the plural.

My favorite representation of this ideal was the statement of the simple agnostic Jew who explained why he came to shul. He said, "I don't believe in God. But my friend, Goldberg, believes in God. So Goldberg comes to shul to talk to God, and I come to shul to talk to Goldberg."

A Hasidic teaching tells us that the name for God is formed when two *yuds* are put together. The letter *Yud* also stands for a Jew *(Yid).* In other words when *yidden* (Jews) stand together, we find God and bring his presence into the world. So let us make prayer a part of our routine and thereby bring God into our lives.

Yom Kippur
5754 / 1993

God Is In the Whirlwind: Tsunamis, Typhoons and Other "Acts of God"

Up until a few weeks ago probably the only people among us who knew the meaning of the word "tsunami" were those who had taken an oceanography class at some point in their lives. After the recent destruction and devastation, we now all know the meaning of the word and of the harm it can cause.

I am tempted to say that you would have to be on a remote, deserted Southeast Asian island not to know what happened or what a tsunami is; but there you would know, in fact, probably better than anyone anywhere else in the world, since that is where it just hit.

The tidal earthquake and ensuing tidal wave caused the loss of hundreds of thousands of lives. It destroyed and literally wiped out whole communities. Thousands of survivors will have to go through the rest of their lives without loved ones and friends who perished in the aftermath of the tidal wave.

The act seems to be of Biblical proportions. We can begin to understand what the Biblical generation that experienced the Flood in the time of Noah must have felt. Words from the Psalms take on new meaning. A Psalm we recite on Friday evening, *Psalm 93*, speaks of the awesome thunder of the oceans, the pounding of the mighty waters over which the omnipotent God sits in majesty.

Another familiar passage from the Friday liturgy proclaims: *Yismechu Hashamayim vetagael haAretz. Yiram HaYam umelo:* Let the heavens rejoice, let the earth be glad. Let the sea and all it contains roar in praise.

In this week's Torah reading we read of the plagues in Egypt as emanating from the will of God. Our torah portion leaves us with the distinct impression that God harnessed the forces of nature in order to teach Pharaoh a lesson. Deriving meaning from natural events is how the Bible and our tradition often responded to tragedy of such proportion and magnitude.

As a result we cannot help but wonder what, if any, is God's role and what, if any, is the theological message of this recent horrific act of nature. The great earthquake of Lisbon in 1755 led many 18th century figures of the Enlightenment, such as Voltaire, to question the existence of a God who would allow such things to happen. How will our generation respond and process these events?

What, if anything, is God trying to tell us?

The Pope has called the tsunami a severe test. Some clerics view its effects as punishment and then seek to ascertain what act or acts could have provoked such a strong punishment.

One Egyptian newspaper has a perfectly reasonable, scientific explanation: the earthquake and huge wave is the result of nuclear tests being conducted in the Indian Ocean with the cooperation of America and Israel, which would not be the first or last time the Arab press attempted to blame the Jews for a natural disaster.

The destruction poses the classic dilemma that has perplexed humans since the time we could think and reason. How could God, who is both omnipotent and benevolent, cause or allow such wanton destruction to occur?

An online poll at Beliefnet.com, a website about religion and spirituality, asked people what role they think God plays in natural disasters like the Indian Ocean tsunami. Five options were offered:

(1) God is punishing us.
(2) God is testing us.
(3) The earthquake and tsunami were sent by God, but we don't know what the purpose was.
(4) I believe in God, but the supernatural had nothing to do with this tragedy.
(5) God does not exist; disasters like this are just forces of nature.

If you believe in a God of both creation and history – a God involved in the lives of individuals and nations and without whose existence our own existence would ultimately have no purpose, you would probably vote for number 3, as did about 1/3 of those who have responded to date.

While online polls are far from scientific, we can note with interest that the answer receiving the most votes, at 51 percent, is number 4, the one that says that God exists but had no connection to the tsunami.

Writing in *The Wall Street Journal,* Christian theologian, David B. Hart, sees in the tsunami only "the imbecile forces of chance that shatter living souls." The Reverend Hakon Langstrom, a Lutheran deacon in Stockholm, tells worshippers, "The God we believe in is not someone who lies behind everything. God did not make this happen."

This approach is similar to the writings of Rabbi Harold Kushner, who proposed such a theory in his vastly popular book, *When Bad Things Happen to Good People.* Kushner wrote that God does not cause the miseries brought on by illness, natural disasters and accidents, and is powerless to prevent them. Earthquakes, cancer, plane crashes – "these events do not reflect God's choices," he wrote. "They happen at random, and randomness is another name for chaos. . . Chaos is evil. . .because by causing tragedies at random, it prevents people from believing in God's goodness."

Directly pointing a finger when Pharaoh increases the Israelites' crushing workload, an outraged Moses challenges God, "Why have you done evil to this people?" When the blameless Job is afflicted with horrific suffering, he repeatedly demands to know why it is happening: "I speak out in the bitterness of my soul," he cries to God. "Tell me why you contend with me. . .Does it befit you to plunder?"

Elie Wiesel tells a story of three rabbis in Auschwitz who convened a court of law and put God on trial for allowing children to be slaughtered. At the end of the trial, which stretched over several days, they pronounced God guilty of crimes against humanity. Then one of the rabbis glanced at the darkening sky. Now, he said, it is time to recite the *ma'ariv* prayer.

In other words it is perfectly acceptable within our faith to question, challenge, express anger and even condemn God – so long as you still believe in God. I believe this response is a healthy one.

Writing in the *Boston Globe,* Jeff Jacoby recounts the Wiesel story and then goes on to write: "To wrestle with God is not to abandon him. To protest against unearned suffering is not to reject his message – quite the opposite. But having protested a seeming lack of compassion and justice from heaven, we are obliged to reach out to the victims and work even harder to establish justice and compassion on earth."

Rabbi Avraham Feder, a conservative rabbi in Israel, wrote about the tsunami in the *Jerusalem Post* that we must recognize that we are part of God's creation and that creation is generally a blessing for us. Although creation can often be lethal, our reaction should motivate and mobilize us as believers to offer to help God increase the blessings.

In the book of Deuteronomy Moses tells the people that God has created a world in which humans are presented with the option of making choices, a world in which we can choose either blessings or curses, good or evil, life or death. This book instructs us with the Godly injunction: *"uvecharta bechayim:* Therefore, choose life!"

We come away from this newest disaster with a sense of humility in the face of the awesome power and might of nature. The event reminds us of the fickleness as well as of the preciousness of life, which can end in an instant. We have heard stories of the seemingly arbitrary nature of instances where one individual was spared, while a loved one was not.

While the news media has done a superb job of bringing us factual information about this story, in the face of all this we inevitably turn to our religious traditions to help to find and understand the meaning behind these events and cope with their impact.

The Torah does not disguise the dichotomous existence that human beings face in this life. We soon learn, moreover, that the curses, the evil, and death that afflict human beings are not only effectuated by a morally neutral nature, but also by human beings themselves.

Part of the religious message to so much death is to embrace the approach of Deuteronomy to choose life. Surely our own religion tells us that God does not want us to be the source of death and that acts of terror and destruction are not in keeping with God's will or intent. A by-product of the tragedy is a reminder of what we humans share in common, our common fate and of our power to bring about good; this ultimate generating of good is what we believe to be the will of God.

We are left with the realization that while the theology of Noah may be lacking something sustaining, the alternative of atheism is equally unfulfilling. We can also see the possibility that the vengeful God of the Bible has learned that it is no longer necessary or advisable to punish in so dramatic a fashion. If we reject the notion of such disaster as punishment, we can either still attribute it to being a part of God's world while acknowledging that we may not understand the fuller picture, or we may conclude that God does not interfere in the affairs of His creation and recognize that disasters like the tsunami occur for the natural reasons scientists say they do.

As a believer in God and as a lover of God, but also as one who feels comfortable challenging, arguing, and being angry at God, I do not need to believe that God caused it to occur. For me the critical thing is to shift the focus from "Why did God do this to us?" to "How do we human beings respond to such an act?"

The response of the world to this catastrophe is truly the bright spot in all this horror. The generous outpouring of aid from individual nations and individual persons has been overwhelming.

On Thursday I participated in a conference call for North American rabbis delineating for us the importance of supporting the unbelievable work of the Jewish community, as coordinated by the Jewish Coalition for Disaster Relief. This coalition is an umbrella of 44 North American Jewish organizations, which is the central address and decision-making process for disbursement of Jewish relief aid. The infrastructure includes the Joint Distribution Committee, American Jewish World Service, Magen David Adom, B'nai B'rith Humanitarian Relief Fund and many others. Suffice it to say, we Jews are well trained in the art of rescue and relief operations.

As part of its long-term relief efforts for victims of the December 26th tragedy, the group is working with partner organizations in the region, including the Sanghamitra Service Society in Andhra Pradesh, India, which helps local fishing communities with sustainable development and disaster preparedness. The philosophy behind the group's post-tsunami effort is to seek not just quick fixes, but long-term efforts through collaboration with other regional groups. As a result we, the Jewish community, has joined in efforts to procure fishing boats, nets and other equipment to get people back on their feet. The old adage about not giving someone a fish, but teaching a person to fish is being practiced. Only this time we are not doing the teaching but rather providing the boats, the nets and the equipment.

The Jewish community's outpouring of support for tsunami relief has been extremely generous, something we should be proud of. The amount collected in just a few weeks has already reached over $10 million from federations, the Joint Distribution Committee, national and religious groups and synagogues.

"Everybody comes in to provide emergency relief, and then they all leave and there's nobody left behind to help rebuild the infrastructure," JDC's executive vice president, Steven Schwager commented. "While a portion of our money will go for short-term emergency relief, a larger part of our money will go for infrastructure to leave something behind that the Jewish community can get credit for." In other words, long after the issue moves off the front pages, the local communities will feel our impact, and we will still have people on the ground offering assistance.

Within hours of the disaster, the Israeli

government dispatched more than 80 tons of food, water, medicine, medical equipment, teams of doctors, nurses and body bags to Thailand and Sri Lanka.

In Israel an organization of primarily ultra-Orthodox Jews, Zaka, collects body parts at bombing scenes and after terrorist attacks to ensure complete burial in accordance with Jewish ritual law. That experience has helped them identify corpses faster than any of the other forensic teams that have come to Thailand, making them much in demand by grieving families.

Magen David Adom intends to build a self-standing field clinic in the disaster zone, and this time its workers will be able to wear their uniforms, adorned with a red Jewish star, when they arrive in the region next week. The three Chabad Houses in Thailand have served as crisis centers for survivors of the disaster.

I cannot help wishing that the response of the Muslim world to this tragedy, which has afflicted primarily Muslim regions of Indonesia and elsewhere, would be greater. Muslim assistance pales in comparison to what the Western nations of the world have done. Saudi Arabia has no trouble dishing out hundreds of millions of dollars to fund fundamentalist terrorist organizations or to hold a telethon to raise money to support the families of suicide bombers, but for some reason, this oil-rich nation can only see fit to contribute $30 million to the world effort, about the same as tiny Netherlands. And they have done more than any other Arab and Muslim nation! Peter Bergen of the New America Foundation wrote in this past Saturday's *The New York Times,* "This anemic effort on the part of the richest countries is emblematic of a wider political problem in the Islamic world. For all of the invocations by Muslim leaders of the ummah, or the global community of believers, they typically do little to help their fellow Muslims in times of crisis." It seems easier for these leaders to expend energies to condemn and harm Israel than to actually try to offer real help to real refugees in a time of critical need.

The contrast in reactions to such an event brings to mind the story about the leaders of the world's great monotheistic religions who were summoned by God. He tells them that the world will be destroyed by a great flood in three days. The Pope goes on international television and addresses the world via satellite. He admonishes the non-believers of the world and tells everyone of the extraordinary meeting with God. He concludes his message with a call to the world to accept the word of Jesus and to convert to Christianity in the time remaining so that all will know true salvation.

The ayatollah, recognized as the leader of the Muslim world, is offered the same media venue. Using the international television hookup, he calls upon the world to become believers in Allah and to submit to the teachings of Islam and the Koran.

When it is his turn, the Chief Rabbi of Israel addresses the world and says, "Friends, we have three days to learn how to live underwater."

Our job now is to set aside the discussion of God's location in the whirlwind and immediately harness our resources and energies to offering help and aid. Later, we can sort out the theological implications and message behind the disaster. In the meantime I urge you to contribute to the fund. In this manner we can affirm through our deeds that we choose life and in so doing align ourselves with the goodness in God and in nature.

January 8, 2005

Coping with Fear

In 1933 the world faced the growing menace posed by an increasingly bellicose and well-armed Third Reich as well as the problems of a ravaged economy. Despair, disillusionment and depression were widespread. President Franklin Delano Roosevelt uttered the immortal words designed to reassure a jittery American nation and to restore calm to a tense public, "We have nothing to fear, but fear itself." Winston Churchill played a similar role reassuring his nation during World War II.

What is it about a calming, confident presence that enables a leader to help people overcome their fears? Throughout history, individuals who have been thrust into leadership roles in adverse times have either risen to the occasion or have not been up to the task and have failed.

This is a time of heightened anxiety; the world we know now is significantly different from the one in which most of us grew up. Dealing with the unknown intensifies our fears and makes us feel vulnerable.

No one knows when or where terrorists will strike next. Particularly alarming is the growing array of tools of destruction at their disposal. It is difficult to enter any public gathering without wondering: what a great target this would be for someone seeking to wreak havoc and cause destruction.

David Ropeik, author of *RISK: A Practical Guide for Deciding What's Really Safe and What's Really Dangerous in the World Around You,* cautioned us about fear. Last October during the height of the sniper attacks in Montgomery County and elsewhere in the D.C. area, he wrote an article for the *Washington Post* entitled, *Be Afraid of Being Very Afraid.* He advised, "Fear in and of itself is a risk. . .the stress of fear is dangerous. . .It is a complicated conflict between our natural, self-protective emotions on the one hand, and on the other, the risk that our fears might actually exacerbate the dangers we face."

Frequently the media does not help, as it whips us into a bigger frenzy, not merely disseminating information, but often contributing to and even increasing panic and alarm. Barry Glassner, author of *The Culture of Fear: Why Americans Are Afraid of the Wrong Things,* says that the most widely held and scariest terrorist scenarios begin in the media.

When threatened we have to be careful not to dwell on our situation and become so obsessed that we become almost paralyzed and afraid to act, go out, or leave our homes.

Merely saying, "We have nothing to fear but fear itself" may not suffice to allay our anxieties, but we can learn a great deal from the collective wisdom of our heritage and from the experiences of the generations who preceded us to help us cope with our fears.

Even the most peripheral view of Jewish history reveals the unimaginable extent to which Jews have been exposed to terror throughout the millennia. On Yom Kippur we read the martyrology, which tells the story of how the Romans tortured Jews, especially those who taught and sought to perpetuate Judaism. We recall the courage of Rabbi Akiba who defiantly resisted the Romans and who uttered the *shema* with his last dying breath.

In the Middle Ages people accused Jews of defaming the host, of poisoning wells, of being agents of the devil, of being the devil, of killing Christian children and using their blood to make matzoh. Terrorists censored and burned Talmuds, desecrated Torah scrolls, destroyed and ransacked synagogues, and tortured and killed Jews. In Poland in 1648 the Cossacks unleashed the Polish peasantry to carry out the Chelmenicki Riots, resulting in the deaths of almost 100,000 Jews. With the horrendous emergence of nationalism in the 1800s, many accused Jews of being parasites and the source of all evil in the world. The pogroms of the 19th century led to millions of Jews leaving Eastern Europe to make their way to Palestine and the shores of this country.

Somehow, through it all, despite it all, Judaism and the Jewish people survived. Not only did we survive and bring children into this world, but we also found the ability to be optimistic and to bring a message of hope to the world.

The immortal words Anne Frank wrote in her diary reflect the eternal optimism of the Jewish people. Taking refuge from German storm troopers in an attic and hoping not to be discovered, she wrote,

> "It's really a wonder I haven't dropped all my ideals, because they seem so absurd and impossible to carry out. Yet I keep them, because in spite of everything I still believe that people are really good at heart. I simply can't build up my hopes on a foundation consisting of confusion, misery, and death. I see the world gradually being turned into a wilderness, I hear the ever approaching thunder, which will destroy us too, I can feel the sufferings of millions and yet, if I look up into the heavens, I think that it will all come right, that this cruelty too will end, and that peace and tranquility will return again."

What is the source of such faith? How can a young

person who sees the world around her being destroyed find inner resolve? How did our ancestors overcome their fears and find the resolve necessary to persevere?

We sometimes forget that we have a treasure that offers powerful, eternal insights and which gives ageless advice. That treasure is the Bible.

About to lead his people into the Promised Land, Joshua is told, "Do not be afraid. *Hazak ve'amatz,* be strong and resolute. Do not be terrified or dismayed, for the Lord your God is with you wherever you go." These words are echoed in the 27th psalm, which we read every day in the month before the *Yamim HaNoraim,* the High Holidays.

Adonai ori, v'yishi, memee ira?

> The Lord is my light and my help, whom should I fear? The Lord is the stronghold of my life, whom should I dread?
>
> When evildoers attack me, to slander and devour my flesh, when foes threaten, they shall stumble and fall.
>
> Though wars threaten me, I remain steadfast in my faith. Should war beset me, still would I be confident.

It concludes:

> Do not subject me to the will of my foes, for false witnesses and unjust accusers have appeared against me. . .
>
> *Kaveh el Adonai,* Look to the Lord.
>
> *Hazak ve'ametz lebecha,* Be strong and of good courage. Hope in the Lord!

That is why the rabbis deliberately inserted this particular psalm into the liturgy that is recited from the beginning of the month of Elul through the fall holidays. Facing unimaginable fears with enemies all around, the writer realized that he could find comfort and refuge in steadfast faith in God. During the *Yamim haNoraim,* the Days of Awe, a time of Judgment, we remember that we should approach God as a shelter from the storm.

A similar theme is expressed in the 23rd Psalm in words familiar to many of us:

> *Adonai Roee, lo ehsar binot desheh yarbeetzaynee.*
> "The Lord is my shepherd, I shall not lack. Yea though I walk through the valley of the shadow of death, I shall fear no harm for You are with me. Your rod and your staff, they comfort me."

Ironically, this psalm is familiar and well-known because it is popular in Christian circles. Most do not realize it is a powerful prayer traditionally said not only as part of one's night time regimen, but at a time of loss. The prayer affirms that one is not alone when living in the presence of God.

One of my favorite prayers, the *Hashkivenu* prayer, is recited only in the evening service at the time of day when people feel especially vulnerable and dangerous. It asks God to spread over us the shelter of His peace and draw us under the protective wings of the *Shechina* to shield us from enemies, pestilence, starvation, sword and sorrow, all very real threats.

These liturgical yearnings show that our sages saw themselves accompanied by a God with whom they were in frequent contact. God was no stranger to them, nor was this deity a mere ephemeral concept. They turned to God in prayer, not the way people in a desperate situation do or on an as needed basis, but as a regular part of their daily life. Prayer came naturally to them, and helped to prevent them from being overwhelmed by a sense of helplessness. As the Psalmist said in the

23rd Psalm, "I am not alone, for the Lord is with me." The 27th Psalm expresses the same wish: "One thing I ask of the Lord, to live in the house of the Lord all the days of my life, to gaze upon the beauty of the Lord, to visit in His Temple."

To our ancestors God was a constant part of their lives. God was accessible and always present. God was real. Like us, they had fears. And so they prayed not so much to change the situation or the reality that surrounded them, but more as a means of coping with whatever they were confronting. They knew that they could align themselves with God, and in so doing draw faith, encouragement and the support necessary to deal with life's vicissitudes. We learn from these passages that our sages confronted fear with faith, faith in God.

Nowhere is this more evident than in the Biblical story of the binding of Isaac, Akedat Yitzhak. Before Abraham binds him to the altar and as he is making the journey to the mountain with his father, Isaac asks, *"Hinei haesh v'haetzim, v'ayeh haseh l'olah?* Here are the firestone and wood, but where is the sheep for the burnt offering?" His question lets us know that he knows what is really going on. His father responds with the telling words, *"Elohim yireh lo haseh le'olah, beni:* God will provide the offering, my son." Abraham's response is the ultimate statement of faith.

From his 19th century perspective Soren Kierkegaard in his seminal philosophical work, *Fear and Trembling,* saw Abraham as the lonely man of faith. He wrote, "Faith, therefore, is not an aesthetic emotion, but something far higher, precisely because it has resignation as its presupposition; it is not an immediate instinct of the heart, but is the paradox of life and existence."

Bound to the altar, Isaac is released only at the last possible moment. One of the primary reasons we sound the shofar on Rosh Hashana is to remind us of Isaac's courage as well as of his faith. Hearing the shofar, the story of the binding of Isaac, and these psalms summons us to pray together and take these messages to heart.

Our ancestors, who lived so long ago, had somewhat different problems from those our own families have faced, and yet their lives were not so different. A few months ago I received an email which commented on how different life was just a generation ago. I have slightly modified it, and share it with you:

> "According to today's regulators and bureaucrats, those of us who were kids in the 40s, 50s, 60s and even 70s probably should not have survived.
>
> "Our baby cribs were covered with bright colored lead-based paint. We had no childproof lids on medicine bottles, doors or cabinets, and when we rode our bikes, we had no helmets.
>
> "As children we rode in cars with no air bags or seat belts. Riding in the back of a pickup truck on a warm day was always a special treat. (Not to mention the risks we took hitchhiking.)
>
> "We drank water from the garden hose, and would have thought it silly to buy water in a bottle from a grocery store. We shared one soft drink with four friends, all from the same bottle.
>
> "We ate cupcakes, bread and butter, and drank soda pop with sugar in it, but we were never overweight because we were always outside playing.
>
> "We would ride our go-carts down a hill, only to find out that it had no brakes, a problem we learned to solve after running into the bushes a

few times.

"We would leave home in the morning and play all day, as long as we were back when the street lights came on. No one was able to reach us all day – because we had no cell phones.

"Instead of video games, computers, cable, or internet chat rooms, we had friends. We went outside and found them. We didn't have all kind of after school activities or car pools. We rode bikes or walked to a friend's home. We played dodge ball, and sometimes, the ball really hurt.

"We made up games with sticks and tennis balls, and although we were told it would happen, did not put out many eyes.

"We fell out of trees, got cut and broke bones and teeth, but there were no lawsuits from these accidents.

"Little League had tryouts and not everyone made the team. Those who didn't somehow learned to deal with disappointment.

"Not all students were gifted, talented, underachievers or distracted. Some just weren't as smart as others. Although they didn't do as well on tests as others, they learned to live with the consequences.

"And somehow, this generation, which shouldn't have survived, learned how to deal with failure and success and has produced some of the best risk-takers and problem solvers and inventors, ever."

Yes, the world our children inhabit is very different from the one we knew. When we were children, we did not awaken each day to a color code on our television screen indicating the level of the terrorist threat for that day. But many of us have memories of drills in hallways and recall crouching on the floor next to our lockers or under our desks with our hands covering our heads in the event of a nuclear attack. Each generation must deal with that which threatens its sense of security. While the nature of the threats and the specific responses may change, faith can be constant.

Human life is about much more than just security and personal safety. Judaism helps us recognize that we are members of a people who embraces life and who are accompanied by God.

Each of us faces our own unimaginable fears. What may appear to be a minor nuisance to one person is real to another. The question is how to cope with these feelings. I am not suggesting that prayer will magically alter the outcome of events. Rather, I am suggesting that ongoing prayer engenders a relationship with God. Praying regularly accompanied by a turning to our sources is a helpful response. It is not the only response, for the Talmud cautions us that a person should pray as if everything depends on God, but act as if everything depends on you. But it remains an important option which too many of us neglect.

As Rabbi Yosef Soloveitchik, *"haRav,"* writes in *Worship of the Heart,* "The basic function of prayer is not its practical consequences, but the metaphysical formation of a fellowship consisting of God and man." Prayer creates an intimate dialogue with God.

Our faith can give us not so much a protective shield, but rather a supportive arm that can help us through difficult times.

Natan Sharansky's contemporary autobiography, *Fear No Evil,* takes its name from the 23rd psalm, because reading the Book of Psalms is what gave him the fortitude to withstand a Soviet regime intent on crushing his spirit and the movement he led. Imprisoned and placed in isolation for his leadership of the Soviet Jewry human rights movement, his book tells one of the most inspiring stories I have ever read of courage, defiance and determination. The major weapons the KGB employed against him and other prisoners were fear and isolation. He did not succumb to their tactics because he found comfort and the power to resist through his credence in Judaism. Despite unbelievable pressure and unimaginable tactics his jailers exerted on him to break his will, Sharansky writes how this faith is what allowed him to stay free and to view his oppressors as the ones who were not free. He writes that in his prison cell he would sing the words of Rabbi Nahman of Bratzlav, *Kol Haolam kulo gesher tzar me'od:* The entire world is a narrow bridge. *V'haikar lo Iefached klal:* and the important thing is not to be afraid at all.

Rosh Hashana
5764 / 2003

Spirituality

We Jews are so accustomed to hearing bad news that it may be difficult for us to accept good news, which is why a Jewish telegram is defined as containing the following words, "Start worrying. Message to follow."

But amid all the disturbing things going on in our society, at least one development in recent years is positive. God appears to be "in."

An article in *The Boston Globe* reported that classes on meditation, reincarnation and spirituality had surpassed aerobic classes in popularity.

The first Soviet cosmonaut radioed back to Mission Control in Moscow in the late 1950s that he had neither seen God nor bumped into any angels as he was orbiting the earth. The famous *Time* magazine cover story a decade later proclaiming that "God is dead" seems to be from a different era. On the contrary, a number of major periodicals contained lead stories this past year on the resurgent interest in God. The front cover of several journals featured representations of angels, and I am not just talking about the annual *Sports Illustrated* swimsuit issue.

The *Celestine Prophecy* has been on the best seller list for almost three years. Other books that have recently appeared on the list include *The History of God* and *God: A Biography.* If only God could find a way to cash in on the royalties! He must not have a very good agent.

Whereas, at one time intellectuals, physicians and others looked askance at religion, universities now consider its study a serious endeavor. No longer are theistic explanations of various phenomena considered implausible. A *CNN/Time* magazine survey taken earlier this year revealed that 82% of all Americans believe in the healing power of personal prayer. The article cited a number of studies which seem to validate the connection between prayer and regular attendance at religious services and health. As one medical school epidemiologist put it, "To research the connection (between healing and spirituality) is no longer professional death."

To be sure, charlatans and other opportunists still capitalize on the weaknesses of individuals desperate for help. One such practitioner, for example, has her patients write letters to their illness. Perhaps it is because of the preponderance of so many illegitimate and/or deceptive practitioners that Sigmund Freud dismissed religious mysticism as "infantile helplessness and regression to primary narcissism."

But clearly we are living in an Age of Spiritual Awakening, when people are more open to recognizing religious experiences in their lives than in many decades. Not surprisingly, many Jews are uncomfortable with this trend. Most Jews are suspicious of the agenda of fundamentalist Christians, since so much of what they advocate conflicts with many of the values of American Jewry. Most Jews base their theology on Christianity; they assume that whatever Christians believe must be the opposite of what Jews are supposed to believe. As a result, if Christians believe in an afterlife, then most Jews incorrectly assume that we do not. If Christians believe that God takes a personal interest in the lives of human beings – then we do not. Since Christians eat corned beef with white bread and mayo, then we should not.

Jews express their skepticism about excessive, overt displays of religiosity in a number of ways. When the boat the prophet Jonah was on was sinking and all the other people on the boat prayed to their gods, Jonah did not. He alone was down below sleeping, while all his other shipmates were praying to their gods.

The Jonah story reminds me of the one about the Jewish mountain climber who lost his footing on a very steep and treacherous mountain. As he started to fall, he reached out and grabbed hold of a bush. Holding on for dear life, he called out, "Help! Help!" Suddenly, a deep voice came from above and said, "It is I, the Lord. I will take care of you. You may let go." At which point the guy called out, "Anybody else up there?"

But the truth is that American Jews are very much a part of the trend to introduce more spirituality into their lives. This burgeoning interest transcends all denominations and has even spawned a new movement within the Jewish community called the Jewish renewal movement. An increasing fascination with mysticism shows up in many quarters. I see it in our own community and in conversations I have with individuals who speak of their individual faith in a manner unthinkable just a few short years ago.

At one time the primary concern of most American Jewish organizations was Jewish survival and rescuing Jews from endangered communities. Now, however, these organizations realize that they must also concern themselves with saving the soul of American Jewry. These groups now accept that the only true way to save endangered Jewry is to rescue American Jews from the abyss of uncertainty and ignorance about our beautiful heritage. As a result, the meetings and conferences of most national Jewish organizations and agencies have put this on the agenda and now conduct seminars and session which focus on these issues as well.

Rabbi David Wolpe wrote in the *Jewish Spectator*

magazine a few years ago about this evolution. In the not too distant past God was not real for American Jews. At a time when most American Jews were primarily concerned with making it economically and socially in America as Americans, God was little more than a footnote or an afterthought invoked at brises and other life cycle events. But, as he writes, "To eliminate God from Judaism is to whisk away the substructure of the edifice and hope that it remains standing. It cannot and will not. At its core, Judaism is not a system of historical inquiry, or a quaint attachment to ceremony or even a distinct community. It is a grappling with God, a struggle recorded in sacred texts, in homilies and history, in Torah and tradition. If that encounter ends, Judaism crumbles and will surely disappear."

What then, after all, is the meaning of "spirituality," a word which is so bantered about today?

Arthur Green, in the article on this subject in the comprehensive volume *Contemporary Jewish Thought,* explains spirituality "as an essential value of the Jewish tradition is striving for the presence of God and the fashioning of a life of holiness appropriate to such striving." He points out that the word "spirituality" did not enter the Jewish lexicon until the Middle Ages. Although it primarily was used by Hebrew translators of non-Jewish philosophical treatises, God has always been at the core of the Jewish experience.

Although Judaism prescribes no fundamental way to believe in God, belief in God is a fundamental aspect of Judaism. I find remarkable the way Jews have clung to a belief in God over the ages, in defiance of all practical considerations. King Ferdinand was once asked how he could prove the existence of God. Without hesitation, he responded, "The continued existence of the Jews."

When confronted with adversity is when we cling most tenaciously to our belief. A number of the true stories collected by Yaffa Eliach in her book, *Hasidic Tales of the Holocaust,* illustrate the depth of belief amidst such tremendous anguish.

One woman recounted what happened when the Nazis took her to Auschwitz in 1944. She arrived at the camp clinging to her desire to live, repeating her determination to herself and to all who would listen. She told her fellow inmates she wanted to live in order to find her husband. Somehow, miraculously, she avoided death's clutch at Auschwitz and was herded onto a train to be transported to another camp. As she stood in the crowded cattle car, she struggled to catch a glimpse of the outside, looking for some kind of sign to give her hope. Just then she saw a tiny crack and looked up at the bright blue sky. There in the middle of the sky she saw a straight pure white line. Upon seeing it she was certain that her prayer had been answered. She prayed, "Oh God, just as you gave Noah a rainbow, you have given me this white line in heaven. I now know that I, too, will survive this deluge of blood, for this is a sign from heaven that you have inscribed my name in your Book of Life."

Sure enough, when the war ended and she was making her way through devastated Europe back to her home town, she spotted her husband on a crowded train platform as he was also trying to make his way back home to find her.

She explained what she believed had happened: "In order to survive, you must believe in something, you need a source of inspiration, of courage, something bigger than yourself, something to overcome reality. The line was my source of inspiration, my sign from heaven. Many years later, when my children were growing up, I realized that the white line was probably the fumes from a passing airplane's exhaust pipe, but does it really matter?"

Such is the power of faith and belief in a personal God that can give people hope and nourish the desire to survive even against all odds.

Perhaps that Russian cosmonaut who did not see God in the heavens was confused by the well-known verse from the Book of Psalms, "The heavens declare the glory of God. And the firmament shows His handiwork." If we listen closely to the verse, we note that the Psalmist is not saying that God is in the heavens, but that the heavens are a manifestation and representation of his work.

Indeed, we affirm God is near. As the book of Deuteronomy reminds us, "This instruction (the Torah) is very near (to you). It is not beyond your reach. It is not in the heavens. . .or beyond the sea. . .It is very close to you, in your mouth and in your heart." A heavenly God is accessible to all of us and within our grasp.

Two Hasidim on their way to make their annual pilgrimage to visit their rebbe stopped to spend the night at an inn. As they were about to leave, the innkeeper approached them with a request. He asked if they could speak on his behalf to their rebbe. He and his wife were childless and were anxious to have a child, so he asked them to ask their rebbe to pray for him and his wife. The Hasidim said they would be happy to do so.

They were somewhat surprised, however, when they returned several days later as they were on their way back home, to find the innkeeper's wife wheeling a new baby carriage, singing melodies and telling everyone that they would soon have a child.

They were even more surprised a year later when they were once again making their annual journey to visit their rebbe; for when they stopped at the inn, they found the couple preparing for a bris.

Upon reaching their rebbe's court, they shared the good news with him. Later one of them approached their master and asked with trepidation and even a touch of jealous disappointment, how could the request of this stranger be granted when his own similar request for a child had not been fulfilled. The rebbe simply smiled and said, "Tell me, Shlomo, in all the years that you have come to me for a blessing, did you and your wife ever go out and buy a baby carriage?

Never mind that we Jews are not supposed to purchase things for a baby until the child has been born. The point of the story is to show the power that can come from sincere belief, how faith can have an impact when it is a real presence in the lives of people.

This message of God's accessibility and nearness is reminiscent of the famous response of the Hasidic Kotzker rebbe when asked, "Where is God?" He would tell his disciples, "Wherever we let him in."

The real challenge for us today is to be able to find God amid our affluence and opulence, to let him into our lives along with our possessions. And this may be even more difficult than in the poorer communities of earlier generations.

People sometimes go looking in faraway places for answers. How sad that today so many young Israelis go running off to India in search of spiritual destiny when they can find it right in their own back yard.

This chase reminds me of the elderly woman who set out to meet a great reclusive mystic in the Himalayas. She trekked across mountains for many days on her perilous journey and finally reached her destination. She was told to prepare to meet the great wise teacher and that she would have her own private audience with him the next day. When she went in to see him, she stood before him and said, "Sheldon, come home!"

What many Jews have discovered is that they can come home and find meaningfulness, godliness and purpose right here in our own religion. A couple of centuries ago Rabbi Nahman of Bratzlav said that individuals experience God through the "gates" of their own hearts. He reminds men and women of today that belief and faith are very personal. All we have to do is be engaged in the search.

Illustrating the difficulty of locating the divine is *a midrash* about the angels banding together in opposition to God's decision to form Adam and Eve in the Divine image. Jealous that ordinary men and women would inherit such a spiritual treasure, the angels conspired to hide goodness and truth from the human beings. One angel proposed hiding God's mystery in the highest mountains, while another suggested concealing it beneath the deepest seas. But the shrewdest angel of all counseled, "Men will search for godliness in the remotest of places. Hide it within them. It is the last place they will search for miracles of godliness."

Look around the sanctuary this evening. God is here. He is present in our community. He can be found in all of us and in each of us. The Divine is in you. May our own journey lead us to the synagogue and to our community, in worship and in study. As the Prophet Isaiah said, "And those that yearn for God shall find renewed strength. They shall spread their wings like eagles."

May faith spread our wings like eagles and in seeking God may we find renewed strength and purpose.

Yom Kippur
5767 / 1996

The Problem With "Being Spiritual"

Is the growing interest in spirituality genuine? Is it authentic? Is it truly Jewish?

Both from our own experience as well as from what others have done to us in the name of God, we Jews have learned from history to be suspicious of excessive piety. Too much certainty and confidence in one's own religious convictions often leads to either disastrous consequences or dogmatism, something Jews have always rejected. The assassination of Prime Minister Yitzhak Rabin this past year is but one sorry example of what happens when intense religious fervor is detached from the ethics and ethos of Judaism.

The heightened interest in spirituality has led many to study Jewish sources and has resulted in broader attendance at and participation in services, as well as a deeper commitment to living a life in accordance with the teachings of Judaism.

And yet for many their new found faith remains a private and personal thing. Perhaps a bit too private and too personal and that is what concerns me. They believe in a personal God who reassures, and who is ever present. But this differs from our traditional approach to the Divine, which is more connected to the living community than to the individual. The faith so popular today seems passive and lacks the traditional Jewish questioning and challenging of the Divine, of a God who challenges and places demands on us.

This attitude of not shying away from challenging God is typified by the classic story about the little boy who was swept away to sea and whose mother called out asking God to help. Miraculously, He responded and returned her son to the dry land, only to hear the mother complain, "You know, God, he had a hat!"

Rabbi Arthur Hertzberg has written a powerful challenge to what he considers to be the latest fad in Judaism. Although, as he reminds his readers, he is a traditionalist who has called throughout his career for more Jewish learning and greater religious seriousness, he finds current developments troubling.

Expressing his concern he writes, "The supposed theological revival is not about God at all. It is mostly about the obsession with self." He laments that the interest in spirituality will lead people to pick and choose those parts of Judaism which make them feel good. The essence of Judaism, however, is not just a plan to make us feel better. While Judaism offers comfort to the grieving heart, solace to the solitary and consolation to those in need, this is not all that God or Judaism has to offer.

Faith linked with community and action can play a role in helping to heal a broken heart. Another classical story tells of a rabbi who advised a woman who was grieving over her loss to go throughout her village and collect a story from each person she met. After a little while she became so engrossed in the stories she heard from others that her pain lightened and she found herself bringing comfort to each of those she visited. Only when she started to serve others, rather than being absorbed in her own problems, did she find comfort. What a typically Jewish response! For ours is a community-based outlook.

We come together to understand more fully that we have an obligation to seek more than our own spiritual contentment. We have a duty and responsibility to God to respond to the needs of others. This is the meaning of being a covenantal people, and of our pact with God.

Much about the current spirituality movement is positive, especially since it brings Jews in contact with the traditional sources and wellsprings of our faith. God has always been at the core of the Jewish religious experience. This is what sets Abraham, the first Jew, apart from the rest of his world. From its inception this concept is what distinguished Judaism from the worship of idols that was the predominant world view of that time. Belief in God is what propelled Moses to act on behalf of his people, to stand before Pharaoh as a liberator and later as a lawgiver in the desert. Their encounter with God also transformed the thinking of the prophets.

But, significantly, none of our great leaders or role models kept the message to themselves. They did not seek to find comfort nor became complacent once they heard God's call. They did not retreat from their obligation to others in search only of "inner peace." On the contrary, their personal experience motivated them to go out among their people and to others. They became passionate defenders of justice, pursuers of peace and dreamers of lofty ideals as well as advocates for their people. A midrash is critical of the patriarch, Jacob, for resting on his laurels. A true tzaddik, righteous person is always active and engaged in working to make the world a better place.

Spirituality, especially the intensely personal kind that is separate from the community and that is not part of the Jewish continuum, does not fit the traditional Jewish notion of religiosity. Achieving inner peace has never been a Jewish ideal or aspiration. Our concept of a righteous figure is much more akin to an activist like Mother Teresa.

Our prayers are in the plural, not the singular, a reflection of Judaism's theology. Some of our most meaningful prayers, such as the kaddish must be said in the presence of a minyan so that we do not detach ourselves from our community. To avoid overly demonstrative gestures of spirituality, the Shulchan Aruch, the definitive code of Jewish law, warns against excessive piety by condemning those who bow too low when reciting their prayers.

Describing the purpose of prayer, Rabbi Abraham Joshua Heschel said, "To pray is to take notice of wonder, to regain a sense of the mystery that animates all beings, the divine margin in all attainments. Prayer is our humble answer to the inconceivable surprise of living." What could possibly be more uplifting?

Our sages have taught that we should attempt to hear God's call to us through the voice of our tradition, through the writings and wisdom of our ancestors and then seek to be as God-like as is humanly possible. The 19th century Kotzker rebbe commented on the verse in Genesis when Ishmael is in the wilderness, "For God heard the voice of the lad. Nothing in the preceding verses indicated that Ishmael had cried out. And yet, even though it was a soundless cry, God heard it." To be a Jew is to try to imitate God and to hear the soundless cry of those who suffer.

We could reasonably ask where does our sense of social justice fit in with the New Age spirituality? Some are so focused on their quest to find God that they do not notice the needs of society. Yet the Torah reminds us more than anything else of our obligation to "help the stranger." Leonard Fein has written strongly that "without social justice, there is no Torah."

Jewish tradition is not a tradition of texts alone; it is also the lived tradition of a people, the story of what a people have made of its sacred text and how it has responded to them.

Spirituality cannot be something amorphous or ephemeral. To be authentically Jewish spirituality must be connected to the roots of our heritage: study, communal prayer and action. Last night I quoted Rabbi Arthur Green's article about spirituality. His essay continues, "The style of Jewish spiritual life has always found its common expression in the deed, meaning specifically the commandments of the Torah as amplified by the classical *halakha.*" What we do is important, not just what we believe.

The *Shabbatai Tzvi* movement, which proclaimed him as the Messiah, in the 17th century, continued even after his death. But it was always outside the pale of Judaism. A short time later the Hasidic movement, which shared certain aspects of its fervor as well as its attraction to mysticism, remained within the Jewish fold. What was the difference between the two? Whereas the Shabbateans denied the *halakha* and the need to continue to practice Jewish ritual, the Hasidim maintained that it continued to be a central part of Jewish life. Similarly, the split of Christianity away from Judaism in the first century came when Paul declared the Torah's laws to be null and void.

Spirituality, as important as it is, cannot be devoid of Jewish content, or Jewish living. Jewish sociologist Jonathan Woocher comments, "For Jewish education to be maximally effective, there must be a living Jewish community in which what is being taught is already visible and valued." We have to live our Judaism.

Traditional Jewish sources talk not only about the importance of us loving God, but also about having a fear of and reverence for God. The real concern is not whether or not we love God, but to live our lives so that God will love us.

To be a partner with God means to share in His enterprise, to let God eternally summon us to pursue a course of action, to study our traditional texts and to pray in the context of our fellow Jews. Religion has to bring us closer to the community, not distance us from it. Our *midrash* comments that the righteous have no rest in this world for they are dedicated to working with God to perfect the world.

We must understand the importance of meeting God halfway and of not being passive or complacent.

A story is told of a devout individual who had endured many years of poverty. He approached God in prayer and asked for a winning lottery ticket. He prayed fervently and was disappointed each time he checked and found he did not win anything. This went on for several weeks. Growing somewhat impatient, he called out, "I have been a faithful, trustworthy servant all my life. God, can't you help me out one time." Then suddenly in the middle of the night he got his answer. A voice called out to him, "Give me a break, Hayim. At least buy a ticket!"

Too many people assume that religiosity entitles them to make demands of God. The issue that must concern us is not what we can ask of God, but what does God ask; nay, what does God demand of us? The Hafetz Hayyim wrote, "For the believer there are no questions, and for the nonbeliever, there are no answers." We must do both – ask questions and seek answers.

In conclusion, there is a place in Judaism for

spirituality. But it should not just be self-centered; it should spring from and be nourished by our tradition. Then we will be noble and worthy mirrors of the Divine image in each of us. May we pursue our quest in a manner that brings us closer to God, our heritage and community.

Yom Kippur
5757 / 1996

After the Ashes and the Attack of 9/11

Maimonides explains in the *Mishneh* Torah that the blasts of the shofar are meant to summon us to arise from our slumber so that we may search our deeds and repent. Expanding upon the purpose of this effort, he writes that "those who. . .indulge throughout the year in the useless things that cannot profit nor save you will look into your souls, amend your ways and deeds to give up your evil ways."

But the piercing sound of the shofar evokes thoughts and images of other blasts: the sounds of bombs exploding, of ambulances and rescue vehicles rushing to save lives, the sounds of muezzins – supposedly holy people – calling from their minarets for jihad, the slaughter of nonbelievers. Originally, I thought of this picture to describe what has been taking place in Israel since last Rosh Hashana and to introduce a sermon about Israel. But now these words seem eerily to apply to what happened this past week in our own country, the attacks on the World Trade Center in New York and the Pentagon.

This is supposed to be a day when we celebrate the gift of life, when we Jews recognize the universality of our mission, a time of hope and new beginnings. But feeling the usual sense of optimism this year is difficult. Like you, I have experienced a myriad of emotions this past week: sadness and grief, a sense of loss and shock. We have all shed many a tear as we watched the horrifying images unfold before our eyes. The stories of mercy and compassion shown by so many have moved and touched us, and been a source of comfort and hope.

As a rabbi, I am supposed to offer hope and comfort. But how can I offer a message of faith, hope and human decency in the face of such premeditated evil? And so instead, I, your rabbi, stand before you and confess that on this Rosh Hashana I am angry. I am angry at those who perpetrated such a terrible act. How can anyone, much less *a group* of individuals set out on a mission to attack innocent people only for being citizens of a nation whose essence, ideals and existence this group both abhors and envies. I am upset with those who have irreparably altered our lives and deprived us of ever feeling safe and secure again.

Was there no one, not even one person, among all those who planned this attack, who had the decency to pause and say, "Comrades, this is wrong. Innocent, good people will die, and thousands of families will suffer as a result of what we are planning to do." Did not any of them pause for a moment and realize that they were taking the lives and destroying the worlds of mothers and fathers, of sisters and brothers, and that they would be leaving behind bereaved parents, siblings, children, and friends?

Who could hear the story of Howard Lutnick, CEO of Cantor Fitzgerald, who lost all 700 people who worked with him, and cried as he spoke about the tremendous loss he and each of the families was experiencing and not share his pain.

I read that a number of ministers preached on Sunday the importance of remaining calm and not getting angry. Yet, the more I think about the cruel-hearted, calculated action, the angrier I get. You may think that my strongly negative expressions of feelings would be inappropriate for a religious leader. But it is precisely because of the religious teachings of my faith that I feel such a sense of indignation and moral outrage. Precisely because our heritage teaches me to have compassion for others, because Judaism maintains the importance of caring for and loving all of God's creatures and upholds the value of human life, am I so incensed at such violations of these basic principles. All religions and people should share these principles. As a religious person I am offended that anyone would use religion as a mask for primitive, unbridled hatred.

Despite all the painful moments in our history, Jews around the world still affirm the beauty and value of all life. The Torah reading this past Shabbat proclaims, "I have set before you this day the blessing and the curse, *uvecharta b'hayyim:* therefore, choose life!" Our tradition teaches that all people are created in God's image, *b'tzelem elohim,* and yet we have to come to terms with the fact that some of God's creatures perform these terrible acts in His name.

I am angry at religious leaders who incite hatred and condone such an act. I am angry at the nations which harbor these criminals and derelicts and at the regimes that finance them. I am angry at those who attempt to explain, rationalize and justify these crimes. I am outraged at those who dance in the streets and who pass out candy to children to celebrate cold-blooded murder. I am angry at those who come on American television and speak sweet soft words in English to assuage our feelings, attempting to deceive us into believing that they deplore such acts, but say the opposite when they turn their backs and speak in their native tongue to their people. I deplore the very societies that celebrate and laud these individuals as heroes. I am furious at those members of the news media who underreport, downplay or ignore those demonstrations of support.

These media stars naively overlook the connection between the terror we witnessed last week and the terrorist acts Israel has faced for years.

And I am especially incensed at a world which is silent and indifferent when the objects of attacks are Jews and Israelis. People suddenly realize that since they may be the next target, something needs to be done. What hypocrites! Just imagine if the nations of the world had, since its birth, stood with Israel in a concerted effort and assisted in combating terrorism instead of cowardly worrying about appeasing so-called "moderate" Arab governments.

As many of our nation's leaders and commentators have reminded us, we must be careful not to assume that all Arabs or Moslems condone this terrorism. We Jews understand what it means to be the object of prejudice and must be careful not to assume that people are guilty by virtue of their religion or national origins. We should welcome the support of those who sincerely and honestly stand with America as it mourns the loss of these precious souls.

But, by the same token let this be the time when we hear from the Arab and Moslem community more than their justifiable concerns about the injustice of ethnic stereotyping. Let us hear more than rationalizations attempting to diminish the horror of the crime by discussing the sense of victimization and humiliation, which the perpetrators feel. Rather than merely denounce the attack on America, let Moslem leaders unequivocally reject the tactic of taking the lives of innocent civilians. The sick notion that suicide bombers merit a place in heaven must be renounced by all.

The time has come for a full *"din vaheshbon,"* a soul searching in the Arab and Moslem world; I am hoping for the kind that we Jews did after a single crazed assassin acted alone and took the life of Yitzhak Rabin. Israel outlawed the political party of Meir Kahane because of the anti-Arab sentiments they expressed. This past summer I saw a small article by a Palestinian who had the courage to ask, "What kind of society are we that celebrates sending young children into battle, uses them as human shields, and produces and promotes such hatred."

We must seek change from all the intolerable, hateful, bigoted, anti-Semitic, anti-Zionist, anti-Western teaching and preaching which foments and creates an environment where these acts are incubated and bred. Let us insist that they isolate and purge harmful radical fundamentalist incitement from their society, just as Israel has done.

The Western world cannot continue to be blind to the problem of this venomous hatred which is so pervasive in the culture of so many Arab nations. The number one song in Egypt is, *I Hate Israel,* and it is number one, not just because it has a catchy tune that's easy to dance to. We must help Israel counter more effectively this kind of hatred. So far only one European nation has said that it will no longer pay for the publication of Palestinian textbooks until the anti-Semitic references are deleted, and that was Germany.

I am angry that Israel has had to go it alone for so long, condemned for any response, regardless of how measured, to terrorist attacks against its citizens. America and other nations are allowed to protect their citizens and avenge and fight these acts of terror, but Israel should not?! It is permissible for the United States to defy the terrorists, but Israel is expected to negotiate with them and consent to their demands.

While firmly advocating the zealous pursuit of peace, our Torah does not call for turning the other cheek. That is found in the part of the Bible that was added later and which we did not accept. The Torah says, *"Haba l'hargecha, hashkem l'hargo:* if one comes to take your life, you should rise up and take his first." This is not about anger or even revenge, but about self defense, a tactic which ultimately preserves life.

Can we find no source of hope and faith out of this tragedy? The stories of heroism and sacrifice that have emerged out of the ashes affirm and remind us how good a people we Americans are.

The Talmud tells us that Rabban Yohanan ben Zakkai attempted to reassure his disciple, Rabbi Joshua, after the destruction of the Holy Temple in Jerusalem. Looking at the ruins, he said that deeds of loving kindness will now be the means to draw near to God. His message is not lost on us. The goodness of our society and of our people will prevail as we rebuild and resurrect what no one can tear down.

Those searing, horrifying images from last Tuesday will forever be emblazoned upon our consciences. Indelibly impressed upon our understanding now is the precarious and tentative nature of life. Who among us is not moved and does not feel for the grieving families? This terrible tragedy reminds us of a central theme of the holidays: to focus on what really matters, on those nearest to us and how precious life is.

How heart-wrenching to hear of the calls made to family members leaving one final message of love. No messages about the mail or the errands which still had to be done. When confronted with certain death, the simple expressions of love, encouragement and concern endure. Here are some of the testaments and last words of the victims, of the passengers aboard the doomed aircraft. Knowing they would not survive, they shared their final thoughts with loved ones.

Jeremy Glick told his wife not to be sad, that he loved her, reassuring her that he would respect whatever decisions she made in life, and to take care of their daughter.

Some did not get through and left messages on answering machines. One passenger told his wife to have fun in life, do the best she could and that he would see her again.

Twenty-eight year old Veronica Bowers called her mother from the restaurant where she worked, Windows on the World, the 106th floor, and said, "Momma, I can't breathe. The smoke is coming through the walls." And after a pause, "Momma, I love you." And those were the last words she ever spoke.

As we ask in the *Unateneh Tokef,* a prayer composed during the time of the Crusades when Jewish martyrs had their lives taken: *Who shall live and who shall die, who by fire and who by water*?

The question in the prayer and in these stories reminds us that life is limited, and that we should put our priorities in order. Let us use this knowledge to turn to those near to us – friends, colleagues and family – and put aside the insignificant, petty differences which occasionally come between us. Let us tell them we love them. Hold them close. Enjoy and savor every moment together.

In light of all the senseless loss of the lives of so many good, decent people, how can you feel anything other than anger? Let us channel this anger into a unity of purpose and the resolve to defeat and overcome injustice, so that good will triumph. And let us not succumb to fear, for to do so is to give the terrorists a victory.

I confess to you that in addition to being angry at the perpetrators of such evil, the societies that harbor and nourish them and the world whose policies condone and allow such actions, I am also angry at God.

I know that these terrible people do not act in the name of God, although they try to invoke the name of God and Allah as being on their side. I question how God has allowed all this suffering and these forces of cruelty and agents of destruction to wreak such havoc.

When I hear about the children in Israel who have become orphaned by terrorists, of the innocent individuals killed for no reason other than the fact they are Israeli or American, I find it difficult to forgive God.

I think of the loss earlier this year of a tender faced, bespectacled 11-year old, Dor Hershkowitz, standing over the open grave of his father who was shot while driving his car. Dor asked, "Who will prepare me now for my bar mitzvah?" And then three months later, he stood over another grave, this time of his older brother Assaf, also killed by Palestinian snipers, and cried, "You were like a father to me."

Sometimes when I learn of such barbaric acts and the family losses, I cannot help but wonder if this God is deserving of our prayers and praise.

I am not being blasphemous. Our tradition teaches that God is big enough to accept our anger and even encourages us to question and challenge Him. Abraham railed against God and said, *"Hashofet kol haaretz lo taaseh mishpat?* Shall not the judge of all the earth act justly?" We are entitled to ask the same question.

Rabbi Levi Yitzhak of Berditchev challenged God one Yom Kippur. He stood before his congregation and said to God, "Your people may have sinned by occasionally forgetting to say some of the prayers and doing other misdeeds. But that is nothing compared to your sins. You have separated parents from their children and caused great suffering among your people. So let's just call it even. We will forgive You if You forgive us."

Do not misunderstand me. Like Rabbi Levi Yitzhak and the Jews of old, I will yet love and cling to Him and to His ways. I will continue to pray to Him, believe in Him, teach His message, try to draw you closer to God, and to observe His *mitzvot.* I do all of this in spite of His actions or lack of action.

So, *Ribbono shel Olam,* I ask, no, I demand that You show us Your compassion. Mend Your ways. I am tired of being your apologist, weary of having to defend You and to make excuses for you. We will continue to do our part; we will turn to You in prayer, study and practice our tradition, and show our tenacious devotion to You by performing the commandments and deeds of loving kindness.

I, Yehezekel ben Shmuel, demand that you send healing. Help us to be strong and stay united and remain determined in our resolve. Help us to defeat thine enemies. Give us strength and courage. Let us win this battle against those who hate and cause loss of life, and then, maybe then, I will forgive You.

And if you cannot do all that, then at least help us when we are angry and afraid, so that yea, though we walk through the valley of death, we shall fear no evil, for thou art with us.

Rosh Hashana
5762/2001

The Blessing of a Blessing

You may have heard the story about the man who makes an appointment with his rabbi to make him a Levi. Tactfully, the rabbi says that much as he would like to accommodate the request, this is one thing he cannot possibly do. So the guy offers the rabbi a donation of one thousand dollars. Again the rabbi politely explains that no such ceremony or ritual exists and he cannot help. This goes on for several days. Finally, the persistent individual offers a contribution of one million dollars to the shul. This gets the attention of the rabbi, who begins to think maybe there is a way to accommodate the unusual request.

"Meet me tomorrow at the *mikveh,*" the rabbi tells him, "I will see what I can do for you."

The next day the rabbi meets him and says that upon further research he has found an obscure document indicating a possibility for fulfilling his request. After entering the *mikveh,* the rabbi incanted some verses in Hebrew mixed with a little Aramaic, and pronounced the congregant a Levi.

As the grateful man gleefully handed over the generous contribution to the rabbi, with a little something extra for his services, the rabbi asked why was it so important to him to be a Levi. "Simple," the man said, "My father, *alav hashalom,* was a Levi. My grandfather and his father before him were all Levis, so I have always wanted to be a Levi!"

As we all know, one's status as a "levi" or "kohen," is determined by heredity, and is dependent on one's father's tribal ancestry. The tradition is passed down orally by word of mouth. No national registry or archives officially records these things. Yet, amazingly, DNA research conducted over the past decade has turned up an astonishing correlation of over 80% possessing the same gene of those claiming to belong to the Levite clan. A fascinating story in *The New York Times* a number of years ago revealed that, based on genetic testing, the claim of a tribe in Africa to be descendants of Kohanim was not so farfetched and was probably true.

At one time Levites and Kohanim had positions of honor and performed important tasks in the Beit Mikdash, the Temple. A famous quote by the British statesman, Benjamin Disraeli, reflected this notion. In response to the anti-semitic ranting and raving of a member of Parliament, Disraeli retorted, "While your ancestors were beating drums on some remote primitive island, mine, Sir, were serving the Lord in the Temple of King Solomon."

With the destruction in 70 CE of the Temple, the role and significance of the priests and their assistants was drastically reduced since they could no longer offer sacrifices. Yet their successors memorialized their revered position in several ways. The rabbis who inherited the mantle of leadership determined that the honor of the first and second *aliyot,* when reading from the Torah, would go to a Kohen and Levi. Restrictions upon the Kohanim dating back to the biblical period were maintained, including the prohibition against marrying a convert or divorcee as well as entering a cemetery and various other customs. Traditional synagogues and individuals still observe these practices, while most nontraditional Jews no longer do.

One such tradition going back to the time of the Temple was when the Kohanim, the priests, who are a subgroup among the Levites, would bless the people in the manner proscribed in the Book of Numbers. The Kohanim ascend the bema to offer the blessing known as the priestly blessing, *birkat haKohanim,* also referred to as *duchenen.*

Before the Kohanim bless the people, they first recite a blessing: *Baruch atah adonai eloheynu melech ha'olam, asher kidshanu bikdsuhat shel aharon vitzeevanu levarech et amo yisrael b'ahavah.* It expresses gratitude to God for commanding them to bless His people of Israel, *b'ahavah,* with love.

The last word, *b'ahavah,* with love, was a rabbinic addition to the text. Scholars have frequently speculated as to why the word was added. The Shulhan Aruch tells us that the word was added because a Kohen cannot have any anger in his heart towards anyone in the congregation when blessing them. This prayer reminds us that leaders of the Jewish people must always have love in their hearts for the people of Israel.

The Gur Rebbe of the 19th century noted that those who participate in the ritual may quite naturally feel unworthy. They may wonder, "Who am I to bless this people?" The rabbis instructed the Kohanim to realize that they are merely the conduits through whom the blessing from God is conveyed to the nation. The Kohanim bless the people, not by virtue of any personal attributes, but because God commands them to do it; this is why they must stick to the text, not embellishing it, but echoing the words exactly as provided by the *shaliah tzibur,* the one who leads the congregation in prayer.

The Kohain must not feel unworthy, but must, at the same time, conduct himself with a sense of humility. Humility is a trait so important in Judaism that it is viewed as one of Moses' greatest attributes. One of my favorite jokes about how important it is not to feel too important concerns the prominent rabbi who, one Rosh Hashana, was overcome with a sense of modesty. He threw himself before the Ark and cried out, "*Ribbono shel Olam,* Master of the Universe, I am nothing." The *hazzan* was equally moved and threw himself upon the ground crying out, "Dear, Lord, I, too, am nothing." At that moment as they both were wailing away, the *shamash,* the guy who does all the things the rabbi and *chazzan* don't want to do, came up to the bema and also bowed down before the *aron* and the congregation and proclaimed in an equally loud voice, "I, too, am nothing." At which point the rabbi looked over at the cantor and said, "Look who thinks he's nothing!"

So the first insight we learn is that the blessing must be offered with both humility and with love.

The Kohanim stand barefoot before the *kahal,* the congregation, to recall that when Moses stood at the Burning Bush and God commanded him to take off his shoes. According to one *midrashic* explanation, this was so he would feel the earth beneath him. In order to be a leader of the people one must feel the hurts and pains of the common people, a lesson our religious and political leaders of today should take to heart.

For centuries the threefold priestly blessing has been a part of Jewish and Christian liturgy. Some say these fifteen words form the most famous set of words in the whole Torah. Perfectly balanced, three lines set pyramidically contain three, five and seven words. Each line consists of 15, 20 and 25 letters respectively, and proportionally increases the number of syllables as well.

Rabbi Joseph Hertz wrote in his classic commentary on the Pentateuch, "The fifteen words. . . contain a world of trust in God and faith in God. They are clothed in a rhythmic form of great beauty, and they fall with majestic solemnity upon the ear of the worshipper. The Priestly Blessing was one of the most impressive features of the Service in the Temple at Jerusalem."

The description of G. B. Gray also captures part of the blessing's majesty. "It gives terse and beautiful expression to the thought that Israel owes all to God who shields His people from all harm and grants them all things necessary for their welfare."

The blessing begins with three familiar words: *Yevarecha adonai veyishmerecha, May the Lord bless you and watch over you.*

On the surface this injunction is relatively clear and straightforward. May God bless you, and may God watch over you to protect you from evil as well as from illness, poverty and calamity.

Classic Jewish commentaries view this first blessing as referring specifically to material blessing, for our tradition sees nothing wrong with attaining prosperity and enjoying material success. The challenge today is what we do with what we have and how we use our financial resources. This is why *tzedekah,* giving to others and supporting our synagogues and communal institutions, are so important as tests of what we do with the blessings God bestows upon us.

The classic *midrash,* Sifre, links the first and last word, asking for blessing and protection, rendering a fascinating insight. We ask God to bless us with material possessions, but then we say *veyishmerecha,* meaning, "May He guard us," meaning, may He watch and keep these from possessing us. In other words may He protect us from corruption related to the attainment of material blessing and help us avoid the harmful effects of wealth.

The sages recognized the importance of using money for positive and noble purposes, because as with

Midas, money can contaminate and destroy. We all know too many instances of people becoming consumed by their wealth. Either their character changes, or they lose sight of what is really important, or they become so obsessed with having more or with having what others have that their judgment, values and ability to function become distorted.

Rabbi Abraham Twerski puts it this way, "Inherent in the acquisition of wealth is the danger of becoming greedy, and greed is essentially an addiction to wealth. Just as a drug addict craves ever-increasing amounts of a drug, and is never satisfied with what he has. . .so does the person whose possession of wealth turns into greed become addicted to wealth, and he lives in constant dread, never content with what he has."

So one way to read the opening line is: "May God bless you with wealth and at the same time may He protect you from being harmed by wealth."

The second line, *Ya'aer adonai panav alecha, vee'hunecha: May the Lord cause His countenance, or light to shine upon you and may He be gracious to you,* is an equally simple and beautiful image. It asks for blessing so as to experience the radiance of the divine presence in your life. Or, another interpretation is a request for God to enlighten you so that you can understand the purposes God has in mind for you.

The light refers to the light of Torah, meaning that this plea seeks the blessing of spiritual growth and fulfillment. This line thus builds upon and complements the first line. Material wealth is not enough. In addition to prosperity we seek spiritual fulfillment. Unlike the first part of the blessing which asks for wealth, here we are not asking God to protect us from this wealth or to watch so that it not be taken from us. The light of Torah is the kind of gift that we can and should share, for it both illuminates and enlightens our world, and those who partake of it.

The last word of the line, *vee'hunecha,* may He give you grace, *chen,* expresses the hope that you may be blessed to find grace in the eyes of others. This means that they will not be jealous of you, but will rejoice in your joys and share in your happiness. This prayer asks that the resentment of others not cause the diminishing of your joy.

Combining the beginning and concluding parts of the verse yields this interpretation: May you live in a society where people will admire you for your devotion to God and Torah. In this perspective success is measured by the amount of love of God and Torah a person attains.

The concluding words, *Yisa Adonai panav alecha, vyasem lecha shalom: May The Lord lift up His countenance upon you, and grant you peace,* imply in the words of one of our commentators, "May God heed the prayers of the people and forgive their shortcomings."

The *birkat haKohanim* concludes, as do all our blessings, with the request for peace. Peace is not just the absence of war. It is the harmony and fulfillment felt by individuals as well as by a society, for the Hebrew word *shalom* comes from the word *shalem,* meaning whole.

This is the whole prayer and my analysis and explanation of the Priestly Blessing. Two actions or requests of God appear in each verse, six in all. God blesses and protects, teaching that blessing means protection. We ask God to shine and be gracious, showing that God's shining face results in grace. God bestows and grants peace, indicating that the bestowal of God's favor results in peace.

The blessing itself has no magical power, and yet

it is very powerful. Attesting to its popularity, archaeologists have discovered this oldest known passage from the Bible in amulets dating as far back as the 7th century, BCE.

Writing in the Jewish Publication Society Commentary on the Torah, Jacob Milgrom states, "It mounts by gradual stages from the petition for material blessing and protection to that for Divine favor as a spiritual blessing, and in beautiful climax culminates in the petition for God's most consummate gift, shalom, peace, the welfare in which all material and spiritual well-being is comprehended."

Although today we will invite the Kohanim to bless us using this blessing, part of its potency comes precisely because the words are not reserved exclusively for the Kohanim.

Thinking of this blessing, Rabbi Steven Leder recalls when he was in Sherman, Texas as a student rabbi while in rabbinical school, the community knew him as Rabbi Steven Leder, the pastor from the Hebrew church. One day he visited an elderly member of the congregation married to a Baptist woman, both of whom were too frail to come to synagogue anymore. As he was preparing to leave, the old man asked the rabbi to bless them. For a few moments he was at a loss and did not know what to say, and then he decided to invoke the words of the *birkat haKohanim.* Years later he reflected back on the experience.

"I learned an important lesson in the kitchen that afternoon. We can all bring blessings to people who need them. Blessings require no great sanctuary, marble, golden ark or microphone. All a blessing takes, all seeing God takes, is a little time, a few words with two people locked in the silent struggles of life, seeking meaning and recognition amid their faded pictures. That's all it took, just a little time and a few kind words to say I wished them well."

The words of the priestly blessing are familiar, because they are simple, yet eloquent. Originally a priest from among the people was supposed to recite this blessing, not a stranger, for blessing requires knowledge and loving understanding of the ones to be blessed. You have heard it many times – at a bris, a bar or bat mitzvah, in synagogue, at a wedding, usually spoken by the rabbi. But the truth is anyone can do it, including a parent or loved one.

Rachel Naomi Remen writes about visiting her grandfather's house every Friday afternoon after school. He would light candles and say a few quiet words of prayer. Then when he finished talking to God, as she put it, he would turn to her, rest his hands lightly on the top of her head, and utter words of blessing. He would begin by thanking God for making him her grandfather. As she quietly stood there, he continued speaking softly, mentioning various things to God; he even told God if she had done something wrong, how good she was for having told the truth.

"These few moments were the only time in my week when I felt completely safe and at rest. My family of physicians and health professionals were always struggling to learn more and be more. If I brought home a 98 on a test from school, my father would ask, `And what about the other 2 points?' I pursued those two points relentlessly throughout my childhood. But my grandfather did not care about such things. For him I was already enough."

Her memory and description of these Friday blessings is so vivid that you would think they had extended over a long period of time. Yet I was surprised when I read that her grandfather died decades ago when she was only seven years old.

Many years later when her mother was very old and unexpectedly started lighting shabbos candles, she told her mother about the blessing her grandfather gave her and how much it meant to her. Her mother, she relates, "smiled at me sadly. `I have blessed you every day of your life, Rachel. I just never had the wisdom to do it out loud.' "

There is great power in audibly reciting a blessing for someone we love. In many homes parents bestow this prayer upon their children every Friday night. When each of my children begins a new school year or a new venture, I place my hands over their heads and quietly invoke God's blessing over them. This is the way I send them off – in God's trusting and loving care – just as I do every Friday night, with love and devotion.

But, again, saying this blessing is not something to be done just by a priest or rabbi. Any of you can say it for someone you care about. I encourage each of you to turn to your loved ones, place your hands on their heads and lovingly invoke God's blessing upon them. The true power of being blessed is that we come to learn that we are loved. And maybe that is the real reason the rabbis added the word *b'ahavah:* with love, to their prayer.

Rosh Hashana
5766 / 2005

God Will Understand: How Can You Be So Sure?

Cardinal Ratzinger invited the chief rabbi of Rome to be his guest at the Vatican, when he was installed as Pope and took the name, John Paul II. The rabbi expressed his appreciation for the invitation, but graciously declined. Much as he would have liked to be there, he could not attend, he explained, since the ceremony conflicted with the celebration of the first day of Passover.

The rabbi could have tried to justify to himself and his congregation his participating in what must have been an extraordinary event and an unusual invitation. The rabbi could have rationalized that this occasion does not happen very often in one's lifetime, whereas Passover occurs every year. However, he did not make any excuses. He observed the holiday of Pesach at home and in shul instead of going to the Vatican for a once-in-a-lifetime experience.

Faced with a similar choice, I question how most of us would have responded. All too often we attempt to rationalize our actions by saying, "God will understand . . ." Such justification is usually then followed by whatever activity the person wants to do, as in "God will understand if I don't attend services on Yom Kippur since I have to complete this really big project at work," or "God will understand if I don't attend the Passover Seder this year, since I have to study for a really big exam, go to an important baseball game," or whatever.

I sometimes wonder how people can be so sure what God would want them to do and be so certain that

God would want them to violate the sanctity of Jewish law and our most important traditions.

When presented with the dilemma of a scheduling conflict that occurs on a Jewish holiday or Shabbat, what we choose to do reflects our values and our own particular priorities. The next time you aren't so sure whether or not you should take off from work or do something else, instead of assuming God will understand what you do, and that His wishes conform to yours, I would suggest you think again. Maybe your boss, or whomever, should be the one expected to understand if you do not attend an event due to your religious observance and conviction. I know the Pope would understand if you went to synagogue instead.

September, 2006

When Prayer Is Difficult

Tonight we gather together at the beginning of the *Aseret Y'mei Teshuvah,* Ten Days of Repentance, to usher in these holy days. What makes them so special and how do they come to be so infused with a sense of holiness and awe?

I think the answer in part is that we have a basic need to affirm the message of this season, that this is a time of beginnings. As a result we affirm that we and the world can change and can be better.

The sense of renewal is enhanced by asserting that God created the world at this time of year. Some of the prayers speak of God as a shepherd reviewing His flock. Others as if we are clay in the hands of the Creator. Despite these seemingly passive images, our tradition affirms the value of each individual and of our ability to determine our fate. On these days our religion requires us to look at the most difficult of all images and portraits – the self-portrait, the one we ourselves create. The value of the individual derives from the fact that we are created by a loving, caring God.

At this time we seek *teshuvah* or reconnection with those people from whom we have become distanced. In the context of these thoughts about the meaning of this day, I share with you a question recently posed to me. The person wrote:

Dear Rabbi,
I am struggling with the issue of why should I repent, ask forgiveness and try and be a better person when

everyone around me does not try to be a better person? When everyone else around me is full of evil thoughts, words and deed? It is so hard to find it within myself to change and forswear bad behaviors when every day I am confronted with those who act badly against me.

The question is a difficult one. I am sure we can all relate to the feelings of frustration expressed in this letter. We worry whether or not others will accept our penitence. Will they meet us halfway?

We can take some comfort in knowing that the problem is not a new one. The Psalmists grappled with similar feelings. As they sought refuge and strength, they were sustained by their belief in a God who does not abandon the faithful.

Part of my response is that I believe with all my heart that working to be a good person makes us better people. It is not just a tautology. To not be forgiving persons can turn us into bitter people.

In thinking of the value of this effort I offer the example of Sherri Mandell whose son, Koby, was killed by Palestinians in a brutal, random and vicious act of violence. She authored a powerful book entitled, *The Blessing of a Broken Heart.* Sherri Mandell wrote,

> "Less than a year after our son was killed, my husband and I marked our wedding anniversary by going out to dinner. I can't say we celebrated, because we were too sad. When we walked into the restaurant, the smiling waitress with her shiny, black hair had a spirit and effervescence I could only admire. I thought to myself, `She has no idea of the pain I am living with, the weight I carry.'
>
> "As my husband and I ate our meal, we

realized that the restaurant was a perfect place to commemorate what would be Koby's upcoming fifteenth birthday. We wanted to take fifteen poor or disadvantaged people out to dinner to mark Koby's birthday – to remember the dead by bringing joy to the living.

"We spoke to the manager about our plans. He said that he volunteered at a nearby center that helped teens from poor, broken families, and he thought that the teenagers would appreciate going out with us. The idea was taking form almost on its own.

"Originally we hadn't thought about taking teenagers out for a meal, but it made sense. Koby was a teen when he was killed. We thanked the manager for his suggestion. Before he walked away, my husband said: 'Do you know the Goodman family? They live around here, and lost their 16 year old son in an accident. We went to the *shiva,* and I wanted to know how they are doing.'

"The manager then startled us when he told us, 'You can ask them yourself. Your waitress is their daughter.'

"I looked at her, at her beauty and her spirit, and I thought, 'You never know what's going on inside a person.' When she came over to our table, we told her of our loss, and she shared her own.

"As we spoke, I realized how much of life is hidden. We don't see what's inside of people. As we shared our feelings, my husband and I felt less isolated. The pain lifted for a moment. Healing may occur when we reveal what is hidden inside of us. . .it brings us closer to others."

So part of my answer to the person who asked me how to forgive others is to say that we should realize that everyone carries their own burdens. It is impossible to know what is going on inside any other individuals, their aches and pains, their dreams and disappointments. You cannot judge others based upon exterior appearances alone.

The process of reaching out and of opening up to another about what we need or what we wish to change, of being willing to take the chance and express our vulnerability is risky. But these revelations allow for the possibility for healing to begin and can open in a restorative way untapped wellsprings of emotion. Leaving behind such hurts and moving on is an essential part of living and coming to terms with life. This process allows us to unshackle ourselves from the past.

We can learn from the Sherry Mandell story I have shared with you that we each decide how to respond to what happens to us. We have the power to choose our fate and destiny.

I constantly marvel how different people respond to the same situation. Some individuals take a minor incident, blow it out of proportion, and become indignant. "Can you believe that so and so did such and such. . ." is how the telling usually goes. And I have witnessed times when other people face similar offenses or even more grievous ones, yet they do not become upset. They don't allow the incident to get to them or disturb their equilibrium. Needless to say, the latter response is the healthier one. Letting go of anger and acceptance of others for what they are can be contagious and even liberating.

May we use this time in the coming days to reach out to others, to our loved ones, and look for the good that is inside of them. Focusing on the positive can help to ease our burdens. More importantly, this effort helps us discover and actualize the good within each of us and the world. Extending ourselves to better our world is after all a part of what we try to do during these *Aseret Y'mei Teshuvah,* Ten Days of Repentance.

May the days ahead be days filled with *tefillah,* with prayer, with *teshuvah,* turning and returning, and *tzedekah,* deeds of kindness and righteousness. And may the *year* ahead be a year of blessing and peace.

Erev Rosh Hashana
5765 / 2004

Is Idolatry Still a Problem?

The following sermon comes with a warning. I am about to do something which, to the best of my knowledge, has never before been attempted in an American synagogue. You are going to hear a sermon which will include citations from the Bible, the Talmud, the midrash, Maimonides, the Shulhan Aruch and Britney Spears. I caution you against trying this at home – after all, I am a professional, with many years of experience.

Let me go straight to the sage whose wisdom I know you are most interested in hearing, Britney ("Bracha") Spears. Earlier this summer the singer was asked by a reporter about her interest in the study of kabbalah, the Jewish mystical texts. She responded, "I have stopped studying Kabbalah. My baby is now my religion." (The same baby she drives around with on her lap without a seat belt.)

Not that I am concerned about the impact the attrition of such a prominent student will have on the realm of kabbalistic studies. I am confident that yeshivot around the world will somehow manage to recover and sustain the loss. After all, they still have Madonna, and Lindsey Lohan has apparently recently expressed an interest.

Britney's comment deserves consideration today, not because of what she is saying about the Kabbalah, but because of the underlying premise it reveals. Although I may be the first rabbi to analyze and take seriously one of Britney Spears' statements, I would like to suggest this morning that her attitude is worthy of discussion, because it reflects a deeper problem in our society.

To summarize and reiterate, she unabashedly and without shame proclaimed that her child is her religion.

In many respects too many parents idolize and worship their children. What may be a well-intentioned reaction to an earlier generation of parents who were busy with their workload and who may not have doted over us, has led our generation to go overboard in the opposite direction and revolve our world and schedules around our children.

Please do not misunderstand me. It is essential to love and cherish protect, provide, nurture and care for our children.

We err and do them a disservice though, when our attention becomes excessive. The ubiquitous cell phone has contributed to enhanced accessibility and availability, maybe even too much. Psychologists call the phenomena of the always present parent, "helicopter parents," because they hover over their children. They try to prevent anything from happening that would harm or diminish their self-esteem and are afraid to say no to them. We should not be surprised when coddled children think that they deserve everything they desire.

When we make our children the center of the universe and encourage them to think that they can do no wrong, we leave them insecure, unprepared and ill-equipped to deal with the realities of a sometimes harsh world. Children raised in this fashion have little sense of responsibility and usually lack respect or concern for parents, elders or teachers. It is often difficult for them to acquire a sense of independence and they may have difficulty making decisions.

We have confused devotion to our children with making them the object of our devotion.

This sentiment is actually indicative of a more pervasive problem than the phenomena of overindulging our children. It is not just children who have become the objects of our devotion, for one of the problems plaguing our society is that we serve other false gods as well.

A fundamental purpose of the Ten Days of Awe ushered in today is to remind us that it is God we should worship. We sound the shofar to awaken us to the message that God is the King and Creator of the Universe, and the one deserving of our allegiance. Our prayers are modified and passages are inserted into the liturgy to emphasize this notion of God's sovereignty.

In fact, the very origin and raison d'etre of monotheism and of Judaism and the very legacy we have given the world, is predicated upon a steadfast rejection of idolatry in all forms.

When Avraham aveenu founded the Jewish religion, the very first thing that distinguished him from all who came before him was his absolute rejection of idolatry.

The midrash tells us that Abraham was called an *ivri,* a Hebrew, for it comes from the word *la'avor,* which means to be on the other side. While the rest of the world worshipped idols, Abraham had come to know that there is only one true God. As another midrash recounts, he grew up in a home where his father was an idol-maker. One day he put young Abraham in charge of his shop and asked him to watch over the merchandise. His father, Terah, was upset when he returned and saw that all the idols had been smashed. Enraged, he asked Abraham what had happened. Abraham explained that when he had placed food in front of one of the idols, the others got upset and started to fight among themselves.

Abraham's father did not accept the explanation. He reprimanded his son and said, "How can you say such a foolish thing. These are all clay objects made by me. They do not eat, move or do anything."

At which point the young child, wise beyond his years, said, "Ah-ha! Why then, Father, do you worship them?"

It is not an exaggeration to say that Judaism began with the quest to smash the idols and the icons revered by others. The first Jew bequeathed to us the courage not to be afraid to be in the minority and to be willing to take a stand that was unpopular but right and morally defensible.

The battle against idolatry was waged not just by Abraham, but by Moses and most of the major prophetic figures of the Biblical period. Elijah stood at the mountain, where he resoundingly defeated and publicly humiliated Ba'al and his prophets. The psalmists mocked those whose gods were made by men as having "eyes, yet they cannot see; ears, yet they cannot hear." The prophets were appalled by the immorality and lack of concern for human life, which stemmed from idolatry. But the prophets did not just fight outsiders. They also engaged in an ongoing campaign against encroachments of idolatry amongst the Israelites, lest they be tempted to adopt and embrace their ways.

The temptation to drift away from God goes back to our inception as a people. Shortly after leaving Egypt and experiencing the miracles of the plagues and crossing the Red Sea, the children of Israel built a Golden Calf. The sight of such a defiant act was so repugnant to Moshe Rabbeinu that he smashed the Tablets of the Law at the foot of Mt. Sinai. Literally and figuratively, he could not bear in his arms the very tablets that asserted belief in one God, while the Israelites were paying homage to another god. The *Meshech Chochmah,* an early 20th century commentary understood that Moses broke the tablets because he did not want the people to think that any object other than God is intrinsically holy.

The powerful opening words of the first of the Ten Commandments, "I am the Lord your God who brought you out of the land of Egypt. You shall have no other gods besides me" are a clarion rallying cry for monotheism. They are amplified by the second commandment restricting any depiction of images of God. "You shall not make for yourself a sculptured image, or any likeness of what is in the heavens above, or on the earth below, or in the waters under the earth, nor shall you bow down to them or serve them." Together, the first two commandments serve as the foundation for all future Jewish belief and are fundamental principles of Jewish theology.

The rabbis of the Talmud devoted an entire tractate called "Avodah Zarah" to the laws defining and prohibiting worship of idols and foreign objects. In fact, the Shulhan Aruch prohibited Jews from trading or selling to idol-worshippers three days before their holidays, for fear that one would commit the sin of placing a stumbling block before the blind by enabling them to carry out their reprehensible practices.

The messianic vision as described in the *aleinu* prayer, which concludes every service, looks forward to the time when God alone is sovereign and that sovereignty will be accepted by all; to the time when "idolatry will be swept away so that false gods will be utterly destroyed." It concludes by quoting the prophet Zechariah who unequivocally hoped for the day when God would be acknowledged as King over all the earth.

The most articulate and passionate crusader against any form of idolatry creeping into our belief system was the great medieval philosopher, Maimonides, the Rambam, who made it a life-long mission and emphasis of his philosophical and halakhic writings. He was such a pure monotheist, he insisted it was impossible to describe God, for to do so would limit and confine the infinite. He taught that the war against idolatry is the main principle of the Torah and explained all anthropomorphic references to God in the Bible as being metaphors, and forbade them from being taken literally.

Fighting idolatry was an all-consuming, defining aspect of Judaism that ultimately helped to shape our very religion.

You may be wondering why any of this is relevant to us today, since Judaism won the battle and resoundingly defeated paganism, polytheism and idolatry long ago.

Or did it?

Britney Spears is not the only one to make a being other than God the subject of her adoration and adulation, and it is not only children who are worshipped.

Too many of us devote too much time and attention to what she and other stars say and do. The mere fact that her abandonment of kabbalah is newsworthy is of itself disturbing. Why should we care how Britney Spears or anyone spends their spare time?! The way we idolize celebrities and pop culture figures, consuming as much unimportant, inconsequential trivial information as possible about their lives and homes reflects our misplaced values. There was a time when such gossip and consumption of nonsense was confined to one or two papers. Now there are a number of magazines, TV programs and even a whole network whose sole purpose is to report to us on what is going on in the lives of for the most part relatively shallow people. We have *People, Us, InTouch, Entertainment Weekly* and countless other publications to satiate our voyeuristic tendencies and to chronicle everything that famous people are doing and their likes and dislikes. How important is it for us to know so many details, and how much more do we really need to know about the antics of Jessica Simpson, Tom Cruise, Jennifer Anniston, Paris Hilton, Sean Penn, Nicole Richie, Brad Pitt and Angelina Jollie? (Ok, so maybe a little more about Angelina Jollie might not be so bad.) Sports figures, movie stars, models and recording artists have become the focus of so much of the media's attention. Is it any coincidence that the most popular show on television today is called, "American Idol"?

The inordinate amount of time spent on hero worship of celebrities may appear to be relatively harmless and inconsequential. But idolatry is not a victimless crime. The Biblical war against idolatry was so intense because it was recognized as a tragic sin of betrayal and disloyalty, of abandoning God, which led to unfortunate consequences.

The Talmud and medieval commentators determined that for violations of any one of three mitzvoth one should sacrifice his own life rather than commit a sin. The three inviolable commandments were performing a prohibited sex act, such as adultery or incest, murder, and idolatry.

These three acts were so fundamental to what it means to be a Jew that people died rather than commit them. The Talmud says that if an emperor is wearing a graven image and then says to you to bow down publicly to him, even if he says you can appear to be tying your shoe, it is prohibited to do so.

Why this adamant rejection of idolatry?

Part of it is motivated by concern over whether the center of existence rests within one's own self, or with God. The sages abhorred idol worship, because they perceived it to be little more than a projected and objectified extension of the self. They preferred a God-centered perspective to a self-centered one, asserting that we are created *b'tzelem Elohim,* in the image of God, not the other way around.

Our High Holiday prayer book, the *Mahzor,* portrays idolatry as the root source of sin and wrongdoing. Elsewhere, the prayer book says the question is not whether or not to have faith, but what kind of faith will we have and what we do or do not believe in.

I am reminded of the joke about the Scottish atheist who was fishing, when suddenly his boat was capsized by the Loch Ness monster. Just as the Loch Ness monster was about to open its mouth to swallow him, this confirmed atheist started praying and crying out to God for help. A booming voice came out from heaven, saying, "I thought you didn't believe in me." And the man terrified by what faced him says, "Come on, God. Give me a break. Two minutes ago I didn't believe in the Loch Ness monster either."

On this Day of Judgment, we make choices, and the choice before us is: who is the god we will worship, serve and revere? Some of us mistakenly place all of our faith in technology, modernity or other panaceas in a quest for instant gratification. Will we turn the objects we crave and long for into gods? In other words, will we be guilty of the very sin our tradition sought to purge from the world?

A story in the midrash has a gentile pose a

question to a rabbi and ask, "If God is so opposed to people worshipping the sun, the stars and the moon, then why doesn't He just destroy them?" The rabbi explains that these and other objects in the world are here for us to use and enjoy, but not to falsely place our faith in them. The challenge is to use them wisely.

Whether you choose to pursue a life that seeks to live in harmony with the demands of a God who calls upon humans to live moral lives or to devote your energy to serving other gods will determine your priorities. We are reminded on Rosh Hashana that the choice is between faith in the Creator of the Universe and the creations of human hands. Our sages viewed this decision as the primary decision of life for they felt that if we do not decide for God we become beholden to other gods. What you decide will have an impact on the other choices you will make this coming year. It will define the kind of person you are and the kind of life you lead, for our belief system determines not just what we express, but what we profess and how we act.

Much of our hero worship and interest in famous people reflects our envy of their lifestyle and material possessions. Consequently, in addition to being cautious not to make celebrities the objects of our admiration, we must be careful not to make the pursuit of material things our religion. Our homes, our cars, our clothes, can easily become all-consuming and overtake our lives. Placing too much importance on objects and acquiring possessions can place an impediment in the path to God. It is easy to become enslaved to the Almighty dollar instead of seeking to fulfill the will of the Almighty God.

We live in a world in which the idolatry our religion opposed for so long has been defeated. Today the threat to our identity comes from a different form of idolatry – the challenge of material secularism, coupled with a lack of meaning and purpose. This day we come to synagogue to align ourselves to the teachings of our faith and tradition and to reaffirm what values should be important for us.

Adonai is close and immanent. At the same time Adonai transcends everything and is beyond our reach. Despite all this, God is One, a unifying and sustaining force in the world, who cares about what happens to us and how we live our lives. Faith in *HaKadosh Baruch Hu,* the Holy One, is not intended to be blind adherence to an angry, vengeful God or to justify violence against non-believers. We Jews believe that God does not seek the destruction of infidels or the killing of innocents, but wants us to pursue peace in our world. God is great, because He is the source of kindness, justice, forgiveness and compassion, all characteristics we are reminded this day to emulate and bring into our lives.

What ultimately is it that the Lord asks of us? The words of the prophet are as true today as they were when they were first uttered and recorded several thousand years ago. "What does God demand of you? Only to love mercy, to act justly and to walk humbly with the Lord thy God."

In the coming year may each of us set aside our worship of false gods and instead walk in the ways of the One True God.

Rosh Hashana
September 23, 2006 / 5767

Transforming a Home Into a Place of Holiness

Once again this Rosh Hashana we awaken to a new world, a world different from the one we knew just a year ago.

Technological advances and modem means of communication allow us to witness first-hand the horrible destruction in the wake of Hurricane Katrina. Heartbreaking dramatic stories unfolded in our living rooms before our very eyes. Images of people suddenly rendered homeless, of thousands of evacuees uprooted from their homes and communities, thrust into unfamiliar surroundings, and forced to start life anew cause us to feel and share the sense of tragedy, pain, separation and loss experienced by an entire region of our nation. Uprooted from their moorings, they must cope in new environments without any of the possessions or community they knew. It is impossible to imagine the myriad of issues these people must deal with, including loss of their homes and along with it, documents, possessions, photos, pets, and worst of all, loved ones.

In the aftermath of the flood, many questions are raised, and many are forced to answer questions.

Federal and local officials are called to task for their ineptitude, incompetence, lack of preparedness and slow response. Oil company executives are asked to account for out of control gas prices and exorbitant profits. Engineers and bureaucrats are asked to justify their miscalculations and decisions. People demand that politicians defend their shortsightedness. Rabbis and ministers, theologians and religious leaders are asked to offer explanations, and even when not asked, are ready to rush in with their explanations of inexplicable events, as if they somehow have a direct line to God and can discern and make sense out of an incomprehensible calamity.

Among the theological explanations offered is one by Reverend Louis Farakhan, who is certain that the hurricane is punishment for the United States going to war in Iraq. A Reverend Michael Marcarage claims it was punishment for the annual gay pride events that take place in New Orleans. Rabbi Ovadiah Yosef says it was retribution for President Bush's support for Israel's withdrawal from Gaza, coupled with the fact that black Americans don't study enough Torah. Far be it from me to question the credentials or conclusions of these esteemed religious figures. Although I can't help but notice that the reason for God's actions always seems to correspond to the political position of the individual expressing an opinion.

Theological speculation, and questions about who is responsible or guilty for the tragedy, are better left to theologians greater than me and to the commissions investigating this matter. The more perplexing and relevant question I would like to consider this morning is how do people cope with loss of such a horrific magnitude? How can they repair and put their lives back together? How can they face the future? How will they preserve the memory of the life they once knew?

Living in a post-Katrina, post-9/11 world, we may be forgiven if we assume that we are the first generation to face destruction of such tremendous magnitude and on such a massive scale. Although the world has changed a great deal in the last 2,000 years, our rabbis living in the first century faced a similar sense of loss and destruction. As usual, the wisdom of our tradition offers instruction and guidance for us today.

The world our ancestors knew was turned upside down when they were evicted from their homes and forced to leave everything behind. Taken away as slaves by the Romans, our plight as Wandering Jews began, and what we call the Diaspora, the dispersion of Jews throughout the world, was unwillingly thrust upon us in the year 70 CE, when Jerusalem was invaded, the city vanquished and leveled by the Romans, and the independence enjoyed by the nation of Israel was lost.

The Temple was destroyed by the Romans and the people's primary place of worship stood no more. After the conquest, all that the Jews revered and held sacred was demolished. Even more than that, it was a repudiation and defeat of their entire theological and ontological system, jolting it to its very core, and threatening to rock the foundation upon which faith and public worship had been founded. It is impossible to overestimate the extent of the destruction. The calamity had a devastating impact on both a national and individual level. The Talmud tells of a rabbi walking amidst the rubble and ashes of the Temple and crying as he lamented what he saw. It was as if he was walking through the ruins at Ground Zero.

But in typical Jewish fashion, they did not languish in their suffering. Instead, the rabbis came up with a plan. Although we are separated by over 2,000 years and our world is amazingly different, not surprisingly, their response has relevance and applications for us today. The innovative resourcefulness of the rabbis reminds me of the joke I told a few years ago about the time the leaders of the world's three great monotheistic religions were summoned before the Almighty and told that the world would be destroyed in three days.

The Pope appeared on international television and informed the world of the extraordinary message the three religious figures had just received. He appealed to the entire world to accept Jesus and convert so their souls would be saved. The Grand Ayatollah got on international satellite hookup and proclaimed that now was the time to submit to Allah, and that as the one true religion, all should become Muslims within the next three days. In the interest of FCC regulations of fairness and equal time, the Chief Rabbi of Israel was also allowed to address the world. He looked into the camera and told his fellow citizens of the world, "My friends, we have just learned from God that we have three days to learn how to live underwater."

The rabbis of the first century, known as tannaim, realized they had to teach their people how to live underwater – how to survive in a world in which their Holy Temple, a symbol of the Divinity of God, of His presence on earth, and of the ability to reach Him and the primary means of communicating with the Holy One, had all been annihilated.

What did they teach? What was in the genetic composition of their writings which gave us Jews the will, ability and means to continue? After all, all the other peoples from that same era are no more, yet somehow, miraculously, we are still here today.

For one, the rabbis taught that God's covenant with Israel was eternal. Contrary to what appeared to be obvious to others, and what they might have otherwise concluded, they affirmed that it had not been abrogated. They postulated that the *shechina,* the Holy Presence which hovered over the Temple Mount, had not been destroyed, but had gone into exile with the people and would accompany them wherever they would go.

Furthermore, and even more significantly, they taught that although there was no longer a Beit Mikdash, a Temple where people could bring their sacrifices, God could still be encountered and he would be just as pleased by acts of hesed, deeds of loving kindness. Third, they developed a system of prayer to take the place of sacrifices. Synagogues became the focal point of the community and the place where holiness could be sought and found.

It was almost as if they had their own version of FEMA, a planned response to the destruction of the Temple – only it worked! As a result of their ingenious adaptations, access to God was not cut off, and the community was preserved. Judaism would live!

The synagogue would play a central role in educating its members, in creating a community by bringing people together. But important as it was, they knew this would not suffice. It was necessary to find an even more decentralized place where the ideals and values they articulated and were in the process of developing could be transmitted and reinforced in an ongoing fashion.

In a brilliant move they ordained that the other place to replicate *kedusha,* to find God and to bring holiness into the everyday lives of the people, would be the Jewish home! Whereas the Temple was called the Beit Mikdash, the place where holiness was concentrated, the Jewish home would become *a mikdash me'at,* a miniature place of holiness, kind of like a mini-me of Temples. The home would become a microcosm of the sacred Temple, and instead of there just being a single central repository of sanctity, the whole world would emanate with sparks of the Divine.

Each and every Friday night, two hallahs would be consumed, just as there were two loaves in the

Temple. The hallah would be sprinkled with salt, just as the priests used to sprinkle the sacrifices. Some of these practices are still observed in many of our homes today, and that is the whole point, and why regular observance of Shabbat is so important.

We, no less than the rabbis of 2,000 years ago have the same need to bring holiness into our lives. While we fortunately are not victims of natural disaster or human destruction, our lives are in disarray. We are challenged by rampant individualism coupled with an increasing sense of anonymity and polarization from each other. We live in a rapidly changing world in which technological advances outpace our ability to master the previous invention. In other words no sooner do I finally learn how to operate the remote control on my VCR so that it doesn't constantly flash 12:00, than it is replaced by a new contraption for me to master.

Few of us grew up in homes as nice as the homes we live in, and that our children are growing up in. Terms like modern, contemporary, novel and latest are affixed to products to entice us to assume the product is better and necessary, and therefore, something we must have. Our closets overflow and are larger than the bedrooms in which some of us slept when growing up. Some of our bathrooms could sleep a family of four. Some of us have almost as many shoes as Imelda Marcos. We have a different pair of designer shoes for every sport, regardless of whether or not we play the sport. Yet, despite the fulfillment of our material desires, our hearts yearn for something else. We may add and expand our homes, but the truth is, the bigger they get, the emptier we feel. Our homes may be filled with the finest furniture and biggest and latest television screens, but they are empty of true communication and quality human interactions. We lack the kind of lasting relationships our parents' generation knew.

One of the things the holidays does is bring us back to our roots and our values. It reminds us that life is about more than the latest fad and mode of finding pleasure and material satisfaction.

The question confronting us is how to bring meaning and value into our lives, for even though we have so much, deep down, we know something is missing.

Involvement in the synagogue community, coupled with creating homes filled with holiness is a path that leads to finding the meaning and the fulfillment we yearn for. Jewish traditions, as practiced in our homes, can play a crucial role in conveying a sense of history, values, identity and belonging.

Rabbi David Hartman has written that the family is important precisely because of the role played by parents to connect their children to their past. He goes so far as to say, "Unless people understand the depth of what the family could be, they miss the whole meaning of Judaism." The late Rabbi Morris Adler of Detroit, put it this way, "Judaism begins at home. It doesn't begin at a meeting or a conference or at a philanthropic campaign. It begins in homes where Judaism lives in the atmosphere and is integrated in the normal pattern of daily life. It begins in homes where the Jewish words re-echo, where the Jewish book is honored and the Jewish song is heard. It begins where the child sees and participates in symbols and rites that link him to a people and a culture."

It is the responsibility of parents to prepare their children so they can cope with critical situations, with life itself. A Jewish home is one in which children are taught respect for parents and teachers, and is not focused only on satisfying the child's needs. The family is an instrument of history, a purveyor of memory and values, all of which ultimately fosters independence. This is achieved when we make our homes places of holiness, a *mikdash me' at,* and it is accomplished in a number of ways.

Jewish symbols should permeate a Jewish home. This can include Jewish works of art, as well as ritual objects. It is best when the symbols are actually used, which creates customs, ceremonies and rituals, all of which lead to memories.

The most obvious and prominent symbol is the mezuzah. It is not an amulet or good luck charm, but something far more profound, proclaiming that the family living there is Jewish. Some people have the custom of kissing the mezuzah when they enter or leave a home as a token of love and respect for the ideas and ideals it contains and to subtly show that God is present wherever we go. It further reminds us when we enter or leave our homes and are about to enter into the everyday world that the teachings of Judaism should accompany us and guide our actions whether in our interactions in the work world or in our family.

The parchment, which must be handwritten is what makes the mezuzah holy, and is often as expensive as the actual container. Some of you may know the story about the man who bought a mezuzah for his rabbi when he went to Israel for the very first time. He proudly gave the box to his rabbi and told him, "You know, Rabbi, it came with a little paper written in Hebrew. But since I figured you already knew how to use it, I threw the instructions away."

The simple requirement to place a mezuzah in our homes can teach us a great deal. One of the debates in the time of the Talmud was whether the mezuzah should be horizontal, in accordance with the injunction to repeat the shema when we lie down at night, or if it should be vertical, since the shema is to be recited when we rise up in the morning. This is why it is placed diagonally, leaning inwards, to teach the importance of compromise in family life.

This in turn points to the principle of *shalom bayit*, peace in the home, as something to strive for. While it is doubtful that any of us fully enjoy this blessing, the point is to work for it, to strive to make our homes places where the goal is not just to buy everything on our list, but to make our homes places where holiness prevails, where the voice of God is sought, and words of Torah are spoken.

Pirke Avot quotes R. Yose Ben Yoezer as having said, "Let your house be a meeting place for the wise." His vision is that the home should be a place of education and enlightenment, where sacred ideas and values are transmitted to the next generation. This happens when our homes are not places where we talk *lashon hara* and gossip about our neighbors, and where our conversations consist of more than car pool arrangements, where on Shabbat and other days of the week we converse about the great ideas of our people and the principles of our heritage, and what it means to be a Jew in the 21st century, of the responsibility of the next generation to carry on our tradition, and of their obligations as Jews to work for *tikun olam*. We must expose our children to the excitement of discussing the concepts of Judaism and of the great debates of our people.

We Jews are admired for our commitment to education. But too many people think this refers only to their obligation to provide their children with the means to attend college. This neither suffices, nor is it what our sages had in mind. Our children need to be equipped to understand what Judaism has to say about the great issues of the day. What position might our sages take on various contemporary crises which pull at our society? Do our children have any connection to the weekly parasha, torah reading? Are they taught to be passionate about the fate of their people, and to care about Jewish survival?

An example of a Jewish value dependent upon the home is *hachnasat orhim,* welcoming guests into your homes, for Shabbat, holidays and other occasions. Holidays should be celebrated at home and in the synagogue, with families and friends. Since it sometimes can get complicated, I want to give you a quick, practical and useful compendium of the holidays.

As a general principle, Jewish holidays are divided between days on which you must starve and days on which you must overeat. Though there are many feasts and fasts on our calendar, none of our holidays require light snacking. So here it is – T*he Dieters' Guide to the Jewish Holidays*:

Rosh Hashanah – Feast
Tzom Gedalia – Fast
*Yom Kippu*r – More fasting
Sukkot – Feast
Simchat Torah – Keep feasting
Month of Heshvan – No fasts or feasts for a whole month.
Hanukkah – Feast on potato latkes and sufganiyot, (jelly donuts.)
Fast of the Tenth of Tevet – No potato latkes or anything else for that matter.
Tu B'Shevat – Feast on fruits.
Fast of Esther – Fast
Purim – Eat triangular shaped pastry.
Passover – Don't eat any pastry you would eat on

Purim. Feast on creative variations of matzah.
Shavuot – Dairy feast (cheesecake, blintzes etc.)
17th of Tammuz – Fast (definitely no cheesecake or blintzes)
Tish B'Av – Very strict fast (don't even think about cheesecake or blintzes)
Month of Elul – New Year will be here in a month. Consider enrolling in The Center for Jewish Eating Disorders before High Holidays arrive and the whole cycle starts up again.

On this day when our Torah reading centers on the life of the first Jewish family, Abraham and Sara, the tradition guides our thoughts quite naturally towards our own families as well as our lives as individuals. Our rabbis projected into the future and bequeathed to us an amazing gift. Out of the ashes of the destruction of the Temple came the concept of the home as a place of holiness. It has served us well all these millennia.

I would not be surprised if a number of my colleagues speak today about the lessons of Katrina, of what is precious and truly worth saving, and of what to save and take with you if a home is destroyed, a truly important message. But I want to challenge you on this Rosh Hashana to think about our homes in a different context: how can we transform and elevate our homes into places of holiness, where yiddishkeit, Judaism and Jewish values are found.

The home I am describing may seem unattainable, and beyond your reach. But trust me, it is not. You may feel ill-equipped to create such a place. This is where the synagogue plays a role in helping to teach and reinforce these lessons. Do not expect us to do it all, to be solely responsible for teaching your children everything there is to know about Judaism, but approach it as a partnership. Together, we can make a difference.

Take adult ed classes, come to services, and your homes can become places of ideas where the intellect is stimulated, and Judaism is portrayed as vibrant, dynamic, and important. Are there Jewish books on your bookshelves? Do you subscribe to Jewish magazines, and to our local weekly Jewish newspaper? Do you try to be informed of what is going on in Israel and stay on top of things? Is Shabbat a part of your weekly routine?

I recently reviewed some passages from various *ketubot*. The words in the wedding document used when a couple starts their life together captures their hopes and dreams and expresses the essence of the kind of homes we should seek to create and of the message I am attempting to convey this morning. An amalgamation of the samples provides some inspiring imagery. "The bride and groom pledge to work together to build a home based on a foundation of love and dedicated to the love of God; filled with mutual support, reverence for learning, kindness, happiness, friendship and love; to establish a home imbued with Jewish culture and tradition that embraces the beauty of our heritage; to have a home based on Torah and where the flow of the seasons and the passages of time are celebrated through the symbols of Judaism and the traditions of our Jewish heritage."

May we each, in the New Year, resolve to bring kedusha, holiness into our home, and to make the home we live in a *mikdash me'at*, a place where holiness resides, where the presence of God is felt, and the spirit of our tradition permeates and enriches our lives.

October 4, 2005

The Shema and the Art of Listening

On some level part of what makes the High Holidays so powerful is that it offers the opportunity to connect to congregants we have not seen in a while, to our tradition, to our liturgy and to our family. While this is what pulls us here, the truth is that none of these things is easy.

Ironically, sometimes it may even be easier to be close to loved ones from a distance. Beth Brown lights shabbat candles every Friday night with her mother, even though she lives in Dallas and her mother is in New York. Through the virtual reality program known as *Second Life* they are brought together on the internet. The site, which has almost 4 million users, is a three-dimensional online game in which the avatars of participants interact in a virtual world, buying and selling land and products. It even has a synagogue, Temple Beit Israel, which has several hundred members. I will believe it is realistic when the avatars can nap during the rabbi's sermons and a breakaway shul is formed.

The 33-year old Orthodox Brown relayed to a reporter how emotional it has been for her to be a part of this community. "Once people started coming, I felt deep down inside that this was an obligation to the Jewish people around the world." She feels a sense of obligation and loyalty to her people, factors which also attract us to each other and to the synagogue.

Some may have issues or difficulties with the tradition, with their family or with the prayers and the theology they express. Yet, despite whatever problems we have, we seek each other out and come together this time of year. We come because it is a tradition to do so, and we recognize value in being part of a continuum that is greater than any one of us. We come out of a sense of loyalty to our people, to our heritage and to our ancestors. We come to be inspired, to learn something and to find meaning and purpose in our lives.

By coming to shul, we become part of a praying community.

For many of us, prayer may present its own unique set of challenges. We may wonder what impact there is in reciting a set of words crafted by others long ago. We may ask how is this intended to move us, and who is listening to us anyway? Are the prayers directed towards God, or are they for our ears?

Of all the thousands of words recited on the High Holy days each of us may have a personal favorite. It could be the haunting *Aveenu Malkenu*, or the *Unateneh Tokef*, which forces us to think about our fate and mortality by asking, "Who shall live and who shall die." Or it could be one of the standard prayers of our daily or Shabbat liturgy that moves you. Or your favorite part of the service might be when the rabbi says, "We now rise for the closing prayer."

Pity the poor individual who came to shul once a year, on Yom Kippur afternoon. He actually had the chutzpah to complain to his rabbi about the repetitiveness of the service and said, "Rabbi, you know I consider myself a deeply spiritual person. I come here once a year, but every time I come you are reading the exact same story about Jonah and the whale!"

Tonight I would like to analyze the six words which you probably hear every time you come here or to any synagogue, whether it is once a year or more often, whether it is on Shabbat or a weekday, whether you get here early or come late. It is the most well known of all Jewish prayers, and is said several times at every service. The first prayer we learn as children, it actually is not really a prayer, but rather a statement, a statement of belief that begins with the injunction to hear: *Shema.*

The six words that comprise the Shema have power and meaning that transcend beyond the mere words themselves. The Shema comes from Deuteronomy, the last of the Five Books of Moses. Rabbi Norman Lamm in his book about the Shema says it is "the symbol of Jewish courage, hope and commitment." Traditionally, it is what a Jew says as his last words, before he dies.

Throughout the ages its recital has been associated with proud defiant heroism. It has been a rallying cry, a pronouncement of belief in a Supreme Being who is above all and who cares about the world He has created. The stirring story of Rabbi Akiba, recalled and retold each Yom Kippur, tells how he was tortured and executed by the Romans in the second century. As a means of showing that he retained his belief in God, in decency and humanity and that he did not succumb to those who sought to repress his spirit and faith, with his last breath, he uttered the Shema. His saga is recorded in the Talmud, and is retold each Yom Kippur, as we will recall it again tomorrow morning. All his life he wondered if he would be able to declare his love for God with all his heart and all his soul. He felt content to know that he had fulfilled this supreme act of love.

The phrase was uttered throughout the period of the Crusades and the Middle Ages by Jews who were tortured and persecuted for their beliefs.

With Akiba as their example, centuries later during the Holocaust, many of our fellow Jews who were martyred and murdered defied their persecutors by clinging to their belief in God. They showed their strength and resistance in the face of inconceivable hatred by proclaiming the Shema in the gas chambers, even as they knew with certainty the terminal nature of their fate. *"Shema Yisrael, Adonai Elohenu, Adonai Echad!"* they shouted.

The Shema is a symbol and proud statement, a rejection of the persecutors who sought to impose their barbaric ways on a people who walk with God and whose mission and purpose is to make the world a better place. While the tormentors committed their inhuman acts, the victims responded with this simple affirmation of belief in a moral God. By defying and resisting the power that sought to suppress them, they overcame both the indignity they suffered and attempts at humiliation, and showed that belief in the goodness of man and God is stronger and more powerful than the depravity that is its antithesis.

The Shema is also a statement of courage.

Last summer Major Roi Klein, the deputy commander of the Golani 51st brigade and father of two small children ages one and three, served in Lebanon. Known among his family and friends for his exceptional spiritual and moral attributes, he was an accomplished saxophone player with an infectious laugh. Considered by all who knew him as a sensitive, calm, spiritual person, he was described in the words of one friend as "a modest, humble, honest person, an idealist who constantly demanded more of himself and as one who didn't seem like a fighter."

But when the fate of Israel hung in the balance last year, he knew what he had to do. He returned to Lebanon, where he had survived an intense battle just a few years earlier. Only this time he was not so lucky. During fierce clashes with Hezbollah forces in Lebanon, he noticed a grenade was thrown towards a battalion of his men. Realizing it was too late to protect or warn them, Roi selflessly threw his body over the grenade and absorbed the impact of the blast, saving the lives of his soldiers.

Just before he gasped his last breath, like the martyrs of previous generations, the men whose lives he had just saved heard him muster the strength to proclaim as his last words, "Shema Yisrael." A few days later, on his 31st birthday he was buried.

"By saying the most central declaration of faith in Jewish liturgy," one article wrote, "Klein transformed the meaning of the Shema, which in the Jewish exile was associated with martyrdom in the face of anti-Semitic persecution, into a religious battle cry."

What is it about this prayer that makes it so powerful and compelling throughout the ages?

A Hasidic master claims that we elevate ourselves, and along with us all of creation when we say the Shema, because we are reaching out to the holy and pure. A midrash from Deuteronomy Rabbah uses a comment on the verse in Ecclesiastes, "For there is not a just man on earth that does good and sins not" to associate listening and doing. Rabbi Norman Lamm explains that we often fall short in our actions and that imperfection is the inescapable lot of humanity. Although we often do good, we can never consistently and thoroughly avoid evil. Reciting the Shema compensates for our shortcomings by reminding us of the ideal we should strive to reach. In other words, even if we cannot achieve perfection, the Shema reminds us of one of the overriding messages of Yom Kippur, of the grand and noble capacity of human potential in partnership with God.

The Shema explicitly contends that there are no Gods other than Adonai, the God of the universe, the same God who has a unique covenantal relationship with the people of Israel. The saying from the Hebrew Scriptures affirms the oneness of God and firmly denies the concept of duality and polytheism. But it is much more than merely a mathematical reduction of the many to one.

A number of the classic medieval commentaries point out that the word *echad* means more than just one. It means *unique.* Consequently, the phrase is an expression of the uniqueness of Adonai, of our God. The Holy One is unlike any other living being. One of those unique aspects is the inability to know or fully comprehend the Divine Entity known as Adonai.

Finally, the word *echad* can be related to a concept of the unity to be found in the universe, an idea poignantly explored by the great thinker Albert Einstein. The Ziditchover Rebbe says that when we recite the Shema, we acknowledge that our lives which are normally so fragmented, disconnected and chaotic can become integrated and at one with the rest of the world through the sense of unity with the Creator.

We may each have different interpretations of the subject or object of the sentence, and we may even debate the meaning of the predicate. As Leonard Fein once put it, Jews may not be able to agree about anything, including, and especially, when it comes to our belief in God. But the one aspect of theology upon which all Jews do agree is that God, whether we believe in Him or not, is one.

A story about an assimilated secular Jewish family captures this sentiment. They moved from the city to a small town and enrolled their child in the best school in the area, a Catholic parochial school. To their dismay their child came home after the first day and said, "Daddy, you'll never guess what I learned today. Did you know that God is really three, that there is a Father, a son and a Holy Ghost, and that his son died for our sins?" The distraught father was concerned about what his son was learning. To set the record straight he sat down and firmly told his child not to believe everything they told him in school. To be sure the child understood he looked him in the eyes and said, "Let me make it clear, son. There is no such thing as a trinity. There is only one God, and we don't believe in Him."

Rabbi Zadok HaKohen describes the experience of saying the Shema with full kavanah, with total feeling and being absorbed in the words, as the means of affirming our autonomous selfhood as creatures worthy of standing before the Almighty One.

Although I am focusing my comments on the one line, "Hear O Israel, the Lord our God, the Lord is One", the Shema also refers to the paragraphs which follow it, such as the v'ahavta where each Jew is commanded to love God with all your heart, all your soul, and all your might. The blessings that precede and follow the Shema are an integral part of the whole package, for they express acceptance of the yoke of the commandments and recognition of God as Creator.

Even if you do not currently subscribe to the philosophical or theological implication of accepting the yoke of the commandments, I would nevertheless suggest on this Yom Kippur if you do not currently say the Shema as part of your regimen before going to bed at night, you should begin to do so.

A statement of faith, a triumphant rejection of the persecutors and their ideology, a battle cry, it also holds sway over us as a symbol of Jewish continuity, perseverance and survival as evidenced by the following story, of which there are numerous accounts.

I have read several poignant true tales about Jewish children orphaned from their parents by the

Nazis. In one rendering it takes place at the Warsaw Children's Hospital immediately after the Second World War. In another it occurs in a convent where Jewish children were entrusted to nuns by Jewish parents who wanted to hide and save their children's lives, as the parents knew the fate that awaited them in concentration and extermination camps.

In each version a rabbi who came to rescue Jewish children was told that there were no Jewish children among the orphans. The skeptical rabbi asked to say just a few words to the children before they went to sleep. Slowly he recited the words Shema Yisrael, and as he did, suddenly he heard voices join in with him. The children remembered what their parents had taught them and used to say to them at bedtime. With this simple prayer they ran, embraced the rabbi and were thus reunited with their people.

I want you to ask yourselves tonight, would your children know this prayer? And if they do know it, would they know it because they learned it from you, or because they learned it in religious school?

I urge you, on this Yom Kippur, say it. Say it with your children and say it yourself as well before you go to bed every night.

There is one other aspect of the Shema I would like to raise, which has nothing to do with the deep theological concepts of this prayer, but everything to do with its meaning. I would suggest that beyond the important truths contained within the Shema, and the statement of faith it expresses, there is another element which makes it so significant and which is deserving of our consideration this evening.

Part of its power is the simplicity of the opening word: Shema: Hear or listen.

It calls out to us to listen to the sounds of the

world as well as of those around us.

It may also entail being able to hear and appreciate silence as well. A story is told of a visitor to a small town who joined the locals on the porch of where he was staying. No one said a word, and after awhile he asked if there was a law against talking in the town. One of the men replied, "No, there's no law here against talking, but we have an understanding that no one is to speak unless he can improve on the silence."

One of the problems with our society is that we do not listen. The prolific author Taylor Caldwell once wrote, "One of the most terrible aspects of the world today is this: Nobody listens to anyone. If you are bewildered or frightened or lost or bereaved or alone, nobody really listens. Nobody has time to listen to anyone. Even those who love you the most – your parents, your children – have no time."

Not even people who are paid to listen actually listen. There is a joke about a psychiatrist who was talking with a friend. The friend said, "Mel, I don't know how you do it. How can you bear to listen hour after hour, day in day out, to people pouring out their hearts about their problems to you?" To which the psychiatrist replied, "Sol, who listens?!"

High school and colleges have classes in public speaking, but perhaps what we need are classes to develop our listening skills. There is such a proliferation of talk shows, but maybe what we would be better off if instead there were more "listening" shows.

The art of listening is crucial to relationships, because it means to actually be attentive to the other, to be present to the needs of another person. It means to be tuned into the other, to be sensitive to the predicament of the other person, and not just thinking about what you are going to say next. Martin Buber set out and wrote his famous work about *I–thou* relationships, when he came to realize the potency of listening. He wrote that we must relate to another person, not as an object for exploitation, as an "it," but as a "Thou," a unique and precious human being.

He summed up his philosophy about religion by saying that it entails responding to the call of another. "Above all, listening to both the silent and the spoken voices, when one person speaks to another, so that together they can remove the barrier between two human beings."

Perhaps this is why the Shema is such an important prayer. It calls out to us, almost as if it is shouting out to us, and demands that we listen and take notice of others. It implies a relationship to another.

There is a qualitative difference between the act of hearing and of seeing. Our sages observe and emphasize that it was no coincidence that at Sinai we heard God's voice. We did not see Him. Some rabbis suggest this was because seeing leads to the desire to visualize an image, which could lead to idolatry. This is also why it is traditional to avert one's eyes and not look at the kohanim when the Priestly Blessing is recited, because it is the act of hearing that is the key. Hearing evokes reflection and thought, connection between the two, as well as the effort to follow and obey what was heard.

The Talmud makes a point of using the expression, "Ta u'shma: Come and listen," when it wants us to pay close attention to something, or to prove a point. When the Talmud wants to introduce a definitive conclusion to a lengthy discussion, it says learn from this, using the words, *Shema mina,* literally, *hear from this.*

A famous Jewish saying is that God endowed us with two ears and one mouth so that we would listen more than we would speak.

On Rosh Hashana we come to shul to hear the

sound of the shofar. In fact, the mitzvah is not the sounding of the shofar, but in hearing it. On Yom Kippur we recite many prayers, but the major plea of these days is to listen, to hear and to heed. The beautiful Shma Kolenu prayer is a plea to God to hear our prayer. Yom Kippur beckons us to listen to the voices around us. That includes the voice of God and the still small voice within us.

It is best when we listen with more than just our ears, but with our hearts as well. When God appeared to King Solomon in the middle of the night and offered him any gift he wanted, the wise king asked for a "listening heart."

It is my prayer that on this Yom Kippur we learn the meaning of Shema, to hear – to hear the cry of anguish of the less fortunate among us; to hear the voices of our children who cry out for our love and attention. We need to hear the words of our spouses, friends and loved ones and to become more attentive to their needs.

We need to hear the urgency of the cry to do something about Darfur and injustice in the world, to hear the pangs of hunger of the homeless and the impoverished, and not turn a deaf ear on the needy.

And let us listen, so that we can become better friends to each other. Let us listen so we hear the despair and loneliness of those we care about, the anger and anxieties, the defeats and disappointments of those who express these needs in anguished sighs as well as desperate cries. If we listen well we will even hear the silent cry for comfort and love.

Shma Kolenu: Let us hear, truly hear the voices around us.

Kol Nidre
September 21, 2007

THE SYNAGOGUE

The Synagogue: The Heart of Our People

On these holiest days of the year an amazing thing happens. All around the world synagogues become filled with people who may not have much of a connection to the Jewish community. As a result buildings expand, walls collapse, chairs are added, extra overflow services are set up, parking lots are reconfigured. All kind of machinations occur to accommodate the annual influx.

Why does all this happen? What is it that attracts Jews to synagogue at this time of year in such record numbers?

The synagogue is the heart and soul of the Jewish people, the source of our strength and faith. Creating such a building indicates our intent to bring the message of the Almighty to the world and a vehicle for our survival. The building is a symbol of God's presence in the world, which is why, throughout history, those who have sought to negate and deny God's word and law have always desecrated and attacked synagogues.

When the Communist Soviet government began to crack down against the Jewish religion in the early twentieth century, one of the first things they did was to close the houses of worship, leaving only one, for show, in Moscow. Whether in Istanbul, Turkey, where 21 Jews were gunned down in cold blood a few years ago, or in Hebron in 1929 where young people sitting in a synagogue studying Torah were slaughtered by Arabs, or in Nazi Germany where synagogues were among the first target of physical violence against Jewish property, our detractors as well as our adherents have always understood the central role the synagogue plays in Jewish life. In this country skin-heads or other demented individuals lash out and desecrate shuls and temples seeking to destroy that which represents Judaism as well as putting down morality and justice.

Yet despite these attacks, the synagogue has remained a fortress of spiritual might and power. In fact, no human institution has a longer continuous history.

The source of that strength is the sense of community which the synagogue engenders. The building serves three distinct functions reflected in its traditional Hebrew names: a house of prayer, a house of assembly and a house of study. This place galvanizes people to perform *tzedekah* and deeds of loving kindness. The roles are all interrelated, for study of holy texts is a form of prayer, just as the bringing together of a group of Jews to perform *mitzvoth* is a manifestation of the presence of God.

A congregation is made up of people who come to care for each other and about each other. A Hasidic story about a man who came to an inn exemplifies this trait. He asked about the welfare of Shlomo, a member of their shul, who did not seem to be in good spirits of late. The people shrugged their shoulders and said they were unaware he was having any problems. The visitor then chastised the people saying, "How can you pray with Shlomo and not be aware of what ails him!"

A congregation is composed of individuals and families, of young people and older people, of the weak and the strong – all of whom draw strength and support from each other. The *midrash* likens the Jewish community to a reed. A single reed is easily bent and broken. Yet when held together, many reeds form a strong bond which cannot be broken.

We are required to say some of our prayers in a

minyan. A minyan must be composed of at least ten Jews so that we can draw support from our unity and community, as well as from our diversity. Nine rabbis do not make up a minyan but ten Jews do. We are a people who value being together.

Our generation is not as "Jewishly" literate as those that went before us. We are less familiar with traditional Jewish texts and less comfortable with traditional Jewish practice. As Rabbi Harold Schulweis often says, whereas our grandparents came to shul because they were Jewish, our grandchildren come to shul to become Jewish.

The role of the synagogue has changed and evolved over the years to meet this new challenge. Different generations turn to it for different reasons but, significantly throughout the ages, they consistently do turn to the synagogue. Although some of its activities and offerings may change, the essence remains the same. It continues to fulfill an educational role as a place to explore and express one's Jewish identity and as a place to attempt to put the ideals of our sages into practice. The synagogue remains a place to maintain our roots and to form links with our past as well as the location for celebrating our festivals and personal joys and accomplishments.

A Jewish text, *Or Yesharim* puts it this way: "A Jew in his relationship to the synagogue may be likened to a branch growing on a tree. As long as the branch is still attached to the tree, there is hope it may renew its vigor under favorable conditions no matter how withered it may have become." The attachment sustains us, but to do so we must be attached. We must belong.

Another story is of a man who had never lived his life as a Jew and had never attended or belonged to a synagogue. Neighbors considered him unscrupulous in business and in his personal affairs. He decided he better do something to change his image, so he joined a synagogue. He told the rabbi, "I'm going to change. From now on, I'm going to attend services regularly." The rabbi was pleased to hear the promise, but cautioned, "I'm glad to hear of your intention. But just remember, going to synagogue doesn't automatically make you a Jew or better person any more than going to a poultry farm makes you a chicken!"

A synagogue is not a panacea or cure-all for society's ills or for the wrongs of any one person. The synagogue does not have all the answers. But it is a place where we can come and ask the questions.

A congregation will have its share of disputes and arguments, as any family is wont to have. But we are united by a sense of mission and purpose as well as a set of customs. There is a story about a synagogue that decided with the arrival of a new rabbi to settle a long-standing dispute over how they should recite the *shema*. Every time they would get to that point in the service, bedlam would break out, as half the congregation would stand, and the other half would shout at them to sit down. After not finding anything in the synagogue archives that would indicate the correct practice, the wise rabbi decided to seek out the oldest living founding member of the synagogue to determine the congregation's original practice. He visited one of the founding members, Mr. Bernstein, in his upper 90s, who was in frail condition in a nursing home.

After being warned by the nurse to be careful not to upset the elderly gentleman, the rabbi said, "Mr. Bernstein, I have come to ask you to help me solve a problem. Half of the members of the shul contend that our tradition is to stand while we say the *shema* and the other half argue that we say it sitting down. Please, maybe you can help. Do you remember what is the original tradition of the synagogue?" He was quiet for a few moments, and then he lit up and said, "Yes, that's it. That was the custom."

"What? What was the custom?" asked the rabbi anxiously.

"The custom was that half the people shouted that we should stand, while the other half screamed that we should sit."

While some customs and rituals may divide us, there is much more that unites us. I conclude with a tale about a newspaper reporter who went to interview construction workers building a cathedral. He asked the man on the scaffold what he was doing, and the man explained the nature of his task. He then asked the carpenter what his job was, and the answer was that he was responsible for the woodwork. The bricklayer responded in similar fashion as did everyone else except for the project foreman who said, "Sir, I am building a House of the Lord."

May we never forget that when we participate in synagogue life, we are building a cathedral of the Master of the Universe.

Yom Kippur
5750 / 1989

Building a House of God

This summer I visited the Washington National Cathedral with my children. This unbelievably impressive and awe inspiring edifice evokes a great deal of holiness and reverence. This magnificent building was finally dedicated last summer – 83 years after the laying of the cornerstone by President Theodore Roosevelt in 1907.

For the past 30 years one man, Richard Feller, was in charge of construction. In an interview with *The New York Times* shortly before its completion Mr. Feller said that he had mixed feelings about being just one stone away from conclusion of the project. "To reach this point is exhilarating and thrilling. But it's also very sad. I love this work and it's sad to think I won't be building a cathedral anymore. I can't envision getting up in the morning and not going to build a cathedral."

He understood how fortunate he was because his life had purpose and meaning. He worked on something that was lasting and enduring, and that he knew would outlive him. He had the rare opportunity to build a House of God.

Those of us who have labored to create and establish our synagogue do not always realize how fortunate we are to be a part of a great enterprise and to work for a goal that is greater than any one of us. In the rush to attend meetings and get things done we sometimes forget that we too, are creating a House of God.

It is hard to believe that just three years ago about 20 families gathered to form a synagogue. We literally had little more than a hope and a prayer. In three short years we have grown to over 100 families, created a religious school and adult education programs, hold weekly Shabbat services, and provide a variety of services to our members and the community.

Ever since the destruction of the First Temple, the synagogue and the home have shared responsibility for perpetuating Jewish life as joint custodians of our heritage. Statements from the Talmud reflect the respect our sages had for this sacred institution. "When a person leaves the synagogue, he should not march with hasty steps. But when he goes to the synagogue, it is proper to run." One of my favorites, "If a person is accustomed to attending synagogue and fails to come one day, God inquires about Him." In an age where people feel anonymous, we feel comforted to know that God cares about each of us.

Our open society allows easy access and free entry to the secular world, leading many to question the need for such an ancient institution. In a culture that places an emphasis on the bottom line people may wonder why it is necessary to support a synagogue and what they get out of it. They relate to a synagogue the way they conceive of a hospital or a service station. Like a hospital they hope it will always be there for them in time of need, but do not want to invest anything to insure that it will be. Like a service station they think they can pull in and out to celebrate life cycle events, without realizing that there are obligations incumbent upon members of the community to support communal organizations.

More than once I have heard someone say, "I believe in God, but I don't need to come to a formal service to find Him."

Yes, it is true that you can be a Jew without being a part of synagogue life, but you deprive yourself of spiritual nourishment, enrichment and reinforcement.

The *"bet knesset"* offers us a place where we enter as individuals and become transformed into a community. What is religion if not the source of learning what it means to be human and the source of help for teaching and strengthening our resolve to do what is right.

A person goes to a library primarily to learn and to a concert hall or museum mostly for cultural enrichment. Here we focus on attaining spiritual insights and to receive reminders of the noble message and calling of our tradition. Being here today, I think of the story of the rabbi who met a former congregant who had not been inside a synagogue for many years. He said, "Rabbi, whatever I want to ask of God, I can ask from my home." The rabbi replied, "That may be true. But perhaps God has something to ask of you." We come to synagogue on Rosh Hashana and other days not only to tell God what we need, but also to hear what it is that God needs, what He demands of us. Here we hear God's visions of the way the world should be.

Rabbi Solomon Goldman wrote, "I come to the synagogue to probe my weakness and my strength, to fill the gap between my profession and my practice. . . to restrain the impulsiveness of my heart and check the eagerness of every muscle to outsmart and outdistance my neighbor. I come for self renewal and regeneration . . .to be instructed by the panorama of Jewish history and strengthened in my determination to be free. . .I come to behold the beauty of the Lord, to find Him who put an upward reach in the heart of man."

Indeed, the synagogue our generation has created is not the same synagogue our parents and grandparents knew. Here is where we can discover the meaning of being a Jew in the 20th and 21st centuries. Let's face it, most of us do not know when *Tu B'shevat* is, and we may not even know what it is. Here we come together to learn and to do, to express and to be reinforced in our practice.

Belonging to a community is more important than we can imagine for it helps us define who and what we are. Sociologist and anthropologist, Emile Duke, concluded that the primary purpose of religion in society is not to put people in touch with God, but to put them in touch with each other.

Certain events in the lives of each of us are too significant for us to face alone – joyous occasions as well as sad times. Religion helps to teach us to face life's vicissitudes in the company of others. When we attend services, we are not alone. We are in the presence of others, as well as our ancestors who preceded us and who may have encountered similar situations. Religious ritual and belief cannot avert danger, but can help us face life's trials and tribulations. Prayer may or may not change the world or the course of events, but it can change the way we respond and feel about those things.

In his book, *Who Needs God,* Rabbi Harold Kushner put it this way: "Our place of worship offers us a refuge, an island of caring in the midst of a hostile, competitive world. In a society that segregates the old from the young, the rich from the poor, the successful from the struggling, the house of worship represents one place where the barriers fall and we all stand equal before God. It promises to be the one place in society where my gain does not have to mean your loss. The man worshipping next to you in church may be an insurance salesman or the manager of a rival business, but for the hour you spend together he is not trying to sell you anything or get ahead of you. . .because we all recognize that in this place we are standing together as children of God."

A number of recent studies show results that do

not bode well for the future of the Jewish community. They reveal discouraging signs about the erosion of Jewish identity and commitment and the high rate of assimilation. The synagogue is a tool in the arsenal of Jewish renewal. It cannot replace the family or the home, but as Rabbi Samson Raphael Hirsch, the founder of modern orthodoxy, recognized in the nineteenth century, the partnership between the synagogue and home is what ensures Jewish survival.

A town experienced a terrible drought. All of the crops had withered, the farmers had lost everything, and people worried about starving. Out of desperation they asked the rabbi of a nearby town, who had a reputation as a "rainmaker," to come and pray for rain.

The next day he came to the town center and began to pray. All the people watched and stood in bewilderment as the rabbi seemed to enter into a trance. But when he completed his prayers, everyone was disappointed, nothing happened.

When asked what had gone wrong, the rabbi told the townspeople, "The fault is not with me, my prayers, or even with God. But look at you. The problem is with you. You asked me to pray for rain, but none of you came with your umbrellas or galoshes."

For miracles to occur, you must have true faith. For things to happen you have to believe, and, more importantly, you have to take action to make happen what you desire.

We, the members of B'nai Tzedek, have brought our umbrellas and our galoshes. With faith in the future and in each other, and with a commitment to share the heritage of Judaism, we have labored to create a vibrant and dynamic community. The formation of this synagogue is a defiant response to the depressing statistics about American Jewish life. We have joined together to form a community and have shared happy times and supported each other through hard times as well. This is the essence of our task.

Not too long ago a psychiatrist wrote an article criticizing her colleagues because they only boasted that they had made their clients more assertive or independent. She said she could not recall anyone claiming that they had made an individual more charitable or more nurturing. Those are the values we seek to embrace in a religious institution.

And what about us in this congregation? How shall we define success?

For a number of our members Judaism has started to take on a greater role in their lives than before. A few in their own words, "have attended more services in the last two years than they did in all the years since their bar mitzvah." Some have started to keep kosher. Congregants have formed new friendships and relationships. Many others have taken advantage of our many adult education classes to probe the meaning of Judaism. Some have gotten involved in our social action programs. Our children enjoy coming to services and religious school and are growing up believing that the synagogue is an important, vital and fun part of their life and that Judaism is an integral part of their identity. Our synagogue is fulfilling the crucial role of serving as a generator and reinforcer of Jewish identity.

In this season when we ask God to inscribe our names in the Book of Life, we note that our names are recorded in many places, on many documents and registries; on certificates, credit cards and mailing lists. I hope that our names will also appear on the roster of those who care about and do something for the sake of our people.

But just being a member is not enough. We want

those who belong to this synagogue to be engaged, to be challenged and to grow.

The success of a sermon can be measured by asking what part of the rabbi's message did you take home with you and try to integrate into your lives? What aspect of the liturgy moved you to evaluate what you do and to consider changing your ways, performing *teshuva,* which is the underlying theme of the entire ten Days of Awe? Are you moved to take a class to learn more about Judaism and to attend services, or is Judaism just something for your children? Have you allowed yourself to be open to the message of our heritage, and to incorporate more ritual observance into your life? These are the ways we can measure the success of a synagogue. The responses are what our annual report would convey if we were a corporation.

Too many people join a congregation and expect that that act alone will suffice to offer them inspiration. It will not. Joining and belonging is the first step. The secret is that you must participate for it to do anything for you. Only then will you truly get anything out of your affiliation.

Many organizations often challenge members to bring a new member. But I would like to challenge each member not just to bring another member. Bring yourself! I would like to challenge our members in the coming year to make a personal commitment to take advantage of at least one aspect of synagogue membership on a regular basis. Choose some aspect of the synagogue which interests you. Get involved. Make a promise to yourself to take an adult education class or to participate in a committee. Make a decision to attend services at least once a week or once or twice a month. I assure you that such involvement will make a difference in your life and in the life of the synagogue.

Working for a greater goal may be difficult because it does not offer immediate gratification. You cannot see the results right away. But those who are dedicated and persevere ultimately have the greatest feeling of accomplishment imaginable. The chief architect of the National Cathedral was sad when his work finally came to an end. Herein lies the difference, although the task of building a building may have a beginning and an end, the task of building a congregation is ongoing.

Anyone involved in the workings of a synagogue or any endeavor which entails giving of oneself to others knows how easy it is to feel overwhelmed and burnt out. The cure is twofold – one is to draw upon the resources of religious faith to offer us a source to renew our energy and replenish our faith. In other words, by coming to services and classes we find the sustenance and encouragement we need to persevere. The other part of the remedy is not to lose sight of the dream. We must always keep our eye on the prize.

In 1952 a 34-year-old woman named Florence Chadwick, set out from Catalina Island 21 miles from the coast of California, determined to be the first woman to ever swim this great distance. She had already become the first woman to swim the English Channel in both directions.

The fog was so thick that day she could barely see the boats in her own party. After 15 hours of continuous swimming in ice cold water, she told those who were in a boat alongside her that she could not go on any longer. They tried to tell her that she was not far from reaching the California coast and that she should keep going. But all she could see was dense fog. Finally, after close to 16 hours, she gave up and they took her out of the water. Imagine her sense of disappointment when she discovered that after swimming over 20 miles, she was pulled out only half a mile from the California coast.

When she spoke to reporters later, she said fatigue or cold was not what had defeated her, but the fog. She said, "If only I could have seen land, I might have made it."

We need a facility to house our programs and which will allow us to do even more for our expanding congregation. With perseverance and dedication, just as we have gotten this far in so little time, I have every confidence we will also soon reach that goal.

As the Psalmist once wrote, "Where there is no vision, the people perish." Fortunately we are blessed with members and leaders who have vision.

I hope and pray that this New Year will be one in which the vision and dream of our congregation will continue to flourish; that its members will find enrichment in the spiritual nourishment it offers. May we be blessed with the knowledge that our efforts are truly holy.

Rosh Hashana
5752 / 1991

What Kind of Synagogue Will We Build?

Money Magazine recently published its annual list of the best places to live in America, based on standard of living, salaries, cost of housing and other related issues. Although no one has yet to publish a list of the top Jewish places in which to live, the Talmud lists the criteria which every Jewish community must include for a Jew to live there satisfactorily. The Talmud's list includes a *shochet* (a butcher), a teacher, a *mikveh,* a *bet midrash* (house of study), a doctor and other factors.

The issue raised by the *Talmud and Money Magazine* is what makes a community a desirable and suitable place to live? The rabbis realized that to create a vibrant community Jews need certain institutions to serve our needs and to gather together and not be alone or scattered.

What is the essence of the congregation, the community we are creating? What will be its nature, and how can the rabbis' insights guide us?

To develop a meaningful religious experience is challenging. Gary Tobin of Brandeis University wrote in a recent study entitled, *The Synagogue's Evolving Mission,* that synagogue members no longer view the synagogue as a communal responsibility. Instead, our consumer-oriented society views the synagogue as a provider of personalized services to individuals such as dating services, senior services, 12 Step Programs and a myriad of other support groups.

Rabbi Rami Shapiro concludes, "What they don't want is Judaism. With the exception of training children for bar and bat mitzvah, the vast majority of Jews have little use for synagogue as a religious institution."

But the synagogue has a unique mission as the guardian and purveyor of Jewish life, especially in the Diaspora. At a time when Jewish leaders agonize over Jewish survival and continuity, we should recognize the role that the synagogue has historically played in the ongoing struggle to maintain a Jewish presence for each generation, as well as for the next.

Supportive of this view, Rabbi Alexander Schindler has written that, "Our central responsibility for creating a Jewish future is teaching our children and ourselves how to live real Jewish lives at home. Only the synagogue can meet this challenge. The synagogue is where Jews are made, where the individual soul and the community are joined. It is the place where modernity and eternity cross-fertilize, where the seeds of Jewish identity are sown. Only the synagogue creates Jews – child by child, family by family, minyan by minyan."

What do we expect from a synagogue?

A Doonesbury cartoon portrayed a couple trying to decide which church to join. They are turned off when the pastor they are meeting tells them that he occasionally talks about subjects such as sin, guilt, denial and redemption. They respond, "There is so much negativity in the world. We're looking for a church that's supportive, a place where we can feel good about ourselves. I'm not sure the guilt thing works for us," adding, "On the other hand, you do offer racquetball." And the wife says, "So did the Unitarians. Honey, let's shop around some more."

Some may only be looking for a place which placates one's needs or makes them feel good about themselves. But if the synagogue is not able to inspire us to reach greater heights and does not challenge us to reassess our priorities and perspectives, it will be a shallow, hollow and meaningless institution.

This is the difference between a synagogue and a community center, and between a synagogue and any other club or organization to which we may belong. Our synagogue should serve as a focal point of our Jewish community and reflect our interests and needs. It should aspire, however, to be more than a place to make us feel contented in our complacency.

We convey messages here that we may not hear elsewhere and which we may not want to hear. I have always subscribed to the notion that religion should comfort the disturbed and disturb the comforted. While you can pray at home and can pray alone and God will hear you, by coming to shul you hear what your community needs from you and what it is that God asks of you.

I hope that we will create a community which takes its Judaism seriously. The name used throughout Jewish sources for the Jewish people is not "*Yehudi,* Jew," but rather Israel. This appellation is eminently more appropriate and significant for it implies "one who struggles with God." I hope we will struggle individually and collectively with issues of belief and doubt, of ritual and observance, issues of conscience and of how to apply the ancient teachings of our faith to today's world. Our school, services, social action program – everything we do – must engage us to grapple with these matters.

I envision our synagogue as a place that will challenge us – in terms of our assumptions of what it means to be a Jew, to grow and deepen our commitment to our faith, and to look beyond our own individual world. You may or may not agree with every action taken by the Board or with everything the rabbi says, but let this be a place where we confront in a meaningful way what being a Jew in the modem world means.

Our generation must confront feelings of inadequacy and insecurity in our own Jewish knowledge and uncertainty about our concept of what Judaism is. We know that there is inherent value in our religion. Our challenge is how to pass on to our children a Judaism which we do not fully understand, but which we so desperately wish to embrace and uphold.

Part of the answer is obvious if we look at what is already the focal point of every synagogue.

The centerpiece of any synagogue, where our eyes are instinctively drawn, is the *Aron Hakodesh,* the Holy Ark, which houses the *sifrei* Torah. This is no coincidence for the Torah is at the center of Judaism. It is a symbol of our commitment to study, to live by the commandments and of the eternal presence of God in our midst.

I remember to this day the first time, when as a little boy, I saw the Rabbi bring the Torah out of the ark and parade it through the congregation. Everyone, old and young, gravitated toward it like a magnet. All the people in the pews moved toward the aisle to touch and reverently kiss the *tallis* or prayer book which had touched the Torah. It demonstrates our people's eternal love of learning, an affirmation of the centrality of Torah in our lives and of our respect and reverence for all that it represents.

A legend in the Talmud says that each day God regrets having created the world, and each day a destroying angel is sent forth to make it all revert to chaos. But God changes heavenly rage to compassion and spares the world chaos when He sees His people engaged in study of Torah. Nowhere in the story does it say that study is the exclusive domain of the young. Although many members join a synagogue so their children will learn about their religion, Judaism is not just for children and is about far more than ritual.

When airline personnel give instructions to passengers about what to do when oxygen masks drop, they tell the passengers to first take the masks and put them over themselves – not over their children's faces. Not giving the oxygen mask to your child goes against every instinct a parent has, but you have to first insure your own survival in order to be able to save your child.

Similarly, for Judaism to survive we must first be concerned with our own well-being. We must start with ourselves and our own uncertainties by creating Jewish experiences and memories.

Of the adult experience in the synagogue Rabbi Harold Kushner in his book, *Celebrate Life*, writes: "Fifty-two times a year the Sabbath gives us the opportunity to step off the treadmill of economic striving and scheduling pressures, and redefine ourselves as free men and women, and as members of a family. Every fall, the Jewish calendar offers us days for solemn majesty, days of cleansing and reconciliation, days of remembering to be grateful for the good things of the earth and world. . . Seventy-six times a year, the Jewish calendar calls on us to stop defining ourselves by what we do for a living or what we fill our days with, and asks us to define ourselves by who we are and who we might be."

In other words, to effectively transmit the treasure we must be more than just custodians for the next generation. We need to be practitioners and cultivators. After all, let us not forget that we are a community of more than just parents. Among us also are singles, widows and families whose children are grown.

Recognizing the ongoing tension and debate over whether study or practice is more important, one sage said, *"Talmud torah k'neged kulam:* The study of Torah, outweighs all the other commandments." But another contended, *"Lo hamidrash haikar, eleh hama'aseh:* it is not study but the deed which is the principle thing." The two, the study of good in religion and the practice of goodness in living, are closely related.

One Sunday morning a father was speaking with his child about his participation in a fundraiser for the synagogue. The child asked why didn't he just contribute the money to needy people in Israel? The father did not know how to respond and turned to me for help. I told the child that we need to raise funds to have a synagogue so that we have a place which teaches Jewish values of concern for others and the importance of supporting Israel and the Jewish community.

I hope that our synagogue will be a place where study will lead to greater adherence to and increased practice *of mitzvot* and Jewish ritual in our daily lives. Through encounter with the text and participation in community, we can create an environment which encourages greater observance of Shabbat and *kashrut* values.

The beauty of Shabbat is enhanced by a sanctuary overflowing with congregants. Each member needs to think about making an individual commitment to make Shabbat including attendance at services a regular part of their lives. The self-defining that Kushner writes about is most fully expressed in the context of a full community. Otherwise, coming to an understanding of oneself is like the sound of applause made by a single hand clapping.

Consider what kind of community will someone find who converts to Judaism? Having learned about the importance of Shabbat, prayer, and Jewish activities, will they find at B'nai Tzedek a group which spiritedly practices or merely professes these ideals?

I envision our synagogue as an active, creative place where we will all experience the joy of Judaism.

A friend of mine told me of a young Orthodox Jew he met who shared his view: "You know, if I didn't believe this all came from God, I would leave it in a moment."

On the one hand I admire the man's honesty, and respect his sense of belief, which serves as his motivation. On the other hand, however, I think something is missing for his observance is rote and devoid of any sense of joy or celebration. Compelled to serve his Master, he goes through the motions, oblivious to the potential for inner satisfaction in doing so.

The *Darchei Mussar* suggests that we should not study Torah or perform *mitzvot* only because our ancestors handed down to us the idea of doing those things. We must study the Torah with renewed vigor and vitality every day in the words of *Peninim laTorah,* "as if it was just transmitted directly to you on Mt. Sinai." It is always fresh and new.

Traditional Jewish sources have very little to say about the architecture of the synagogue. But one thing on which they did agree was that a place of worship should have a window to ensure that we are not insulated from the outside world. We must be cognizant that there is a world out there beyond our own. In that vein I hope that our synagogue will strive to be a part of the world around us. We need to take an active role in social action projects and concerns of social justice.

People occasionally complain to me that too often on the holidays rabbis discuss contemporary issues, human sexuality, or whatever is of the moment. I respond by paraphrasing Rabbi Ben Bag Bag, as quoted in *Pirke Avot,* "all is Torah." Judaism has something to say about everything, or it has nothing to say about anything. We must be involved in the community – whether it is helping the homeless or participating in a demonstration on behalf of those who suffer in Bosnia or Rwanda.

We must be concerned with the fate of our fellow Jews as well. A central tenet of Judaism is that the fate of all of Israel is inextricably linked with all Jews. So let our synagogue be a place where we will shed tears for Argentina and its Jews and be inspired by the message of the miracle of modern day Israel. A place where we will be advocates of programs which link us to other Jews around the world. Here we come to understand that as Jews we are obligated not to turn our backs on other Jews but to participate as full partners in the unfolding drama of being a part of the Jewish people.

The Hasidic master, Rabbi Nahman of Bratzlav, used to say that a person should always reach in three directions: inward, to discover his true inner self; outward to reach others and not be alone, and upward to God, the Creator of all. He went on to teach that the irony of human existence is that when we reach in one direction, we wind up encountering the other two.

Similarly, I believe a synagogue should promote this kind of turning. Ours should be an active congregation, one which will have the capacity to affect the lives of its members and their families as well as the ability to change our community and thus create a better world.

One of the stories I frequently told when we first gathered to form a congregation came from the *midrash* about Nahshon ben Aminadav. Although the Egyptians were in hot pursuit, the waters of the Sea of Reeds did not part when Moses held up his hands. Rather, this miracle only happened because of the courage of a single Jew, Nahshon, who was willing to go forward into the water. He had the faith and confidence that the waters would recede and that his fellow Israelites would follow him. He persevered and proceeded until the water was all the way up to his mouth before the sea receded. His is the story of the power of faith coupled with action, or as noted educator, Shulamith Elster recently wrote, "Real Jewish education is not 'learning about' Judaism. It's not reading about Judaism. It is living Judaism. It's not thinking about Judaism. It's doing Jewish things. It's not dreaming about a better world, it's making this world better."

As I am about to conclude my vision of the kind of synagogue we should seek to establish, I have discussed the kind of activities we should pursue, including study, Shabbat, and social action. But I would be remiss if I left out the most important part of all, the fabric of our community. In promulgating Jewish values, it does not suffice to only speak about or teach them, and then not practice them. *Derekh eretz* refers to how we treat each other and instructs us to treat each other with respect and decency. Rooted in the moral spiritual character of Judaism's teaching is the importance of treating each person with the courtesy and dignity due a creature created, *b'tzelem elohim,* or in the image of God. So let us base our encounters with each other, with our synagogue's teachers and professional staff upon *derekh eretz,* for such treatment will be the most important evidence of the kind of synagogue we establish.

Earlier this evening I said that the meaning of Israel is that of one who struggles with God. Israel's late Chief Rabbi, Harav Avraham Kook, had a different interpretation. He taught that it comes from the term, *yashir el,* meaning, "Let Israel be a song unto God."

I pray that the actions of our congregation will be a song, a love song unto God.

Erev Yom Kippur
5755 / 1994

The Secret of the Letters

This year, as is true every year, I agonized over what messages to share with you on these most holy of days. Knowing that our congregation is gathered together for the very first High Holy Days in our new building, I am cognizant of how important it is to share words of insight and inspiration, a challenge that I both dread and welcome. Of what should a rabbi speak on the *Yamim HaNoraim,* our holiest days?

This special occasion reminds me of the story of the rabbi who took a position in a new synagogue. The president of the congregation warned the rabbi in advance that several topics were taboo. "Rabbi," he said, "Don't speak about *kashrut,* because most of our members don't observe the dietary laws. And, rabbi, it wouldn't be a good idea to speak about the Sabbath, because so many of our congregants work and do other things on Saturday. And it would most definitely not be prudent to discuss social action or *tzedekah* since so many people are sensitive and might be offended by these issues." So the rabbi asked the president, "Nu? So what should I speak about?" To which the president replied, "Why, that's easy – speak about Judaism of course!"

What the shul president and far too many Jews do not realize is that Judaism touches upon every aspect of our lives. It cannot and should not be compartmentalized or trivialized by only dealing with subjects we wish to hear or which do not challenge our beliefs and practices.

We can learn a great deal if we begin by focusing

our attention on the sanctuary itself. We chose the motif of the Hebrew alphabet for several reasons. Just as Islamic art incorporates Arabic letters into the artistic motifs of mosques, so should the Hebrew letters, which tell the story of our religion, serve as symbols of the beauty of our heritage, culture and creativity.

The letters contain many mysteries and insights, for the mystics believe that each and every letter has a unique story to tell. The midrash tells us that when God created the world, He created it with the Torah, and that the letters preceded everything. *"Bereshit,* in the beginning, *bara elohim et,* when God created the world He created *et:* i.e., *the aleph* and the *tav."* In other words, the letters were the primordial material used by God to create the world. Consequently, according to the *Zohar,* the mystical commentary on the story of creation, the 22 sacred letters are primal, spiritual forces through which God articulates His will. Each letter has its own magical power.

On Yom Kippur we recount the story graphically told in the Talmud of the courage of Rabbi Hanina who defied the Romans by teaching Torah. When the Romans captured and tortured him, they wrapped him in a Torah scroll, which they then set afire. His disciples, forced to look, stood watching in horror. He called out to them not to despair. Although the parchment was burning, the holy letters were flying upwards, towards God, he told them.

Let the letters remind us, therefore, of the meaning of sacrifice and service, of the fact that they cannot stand, and holiness does not exist in a place of cruelty and repression and that we should always strive to reach the heavens with our words and actions.

The letters on the wall are here to also remind us of another famous Hasidic story about a poor man who entered the shul one Rosh Hashana. It had been quite some time since he had visited a synagogue and he was unfamiliar with what to do. Handed *a siddur,* the Jewish prayer book, he did not know how to read and felt intimidated, uncomfortable and embarrassed. He had drifted so far away from his roots that he had forgotten how to *daven* and how to read Hebrew. All he remembered were the letters he had learned many years ago as a little boy.

Quietly, with tears in his eyes, he recited the letters of the alphabet. As he mumbled the aleph bet, he looked upward and said, *"Ribbono shel olam,* Master of the Universe, I do not know how to pray, I do not know how to read the prayers. The truth is I don't even know how to hold the prayer book. All I know is that my heart longs for You, that I want to pray with my people and with all my heart. I know, dear God, that You, however, know the prayers. So I will say the letters of the alphabet and offer them to you, and then, You, Almighty God, can put them together to form the words of the sacred prayers of our heritage and people."

And the *Baal Shem Tov* added that this sincere prayer from the heart was accepted and reached directly up to heaven.

That is why we place letters on the wall facing you. On this Rosh Hashana we remember that anonymous peasant who so moved the *Baal Shem Tov,* for we are like the poor Jew who comes to shul wanting to pray, but perhaps not knowing how.

The letters of the alphabet serve to remind all who enter our sanctuary that prayer and Judaism is accessible to anyone who takes the first step, to all who come forward with sincerity in their hearts. Together let us open the pages of the *siddur.* Let us explore the stories of the Bible and let us learn the wisdom of the sages here in this synagogue.

As modem Jews at the end of the twentieth century we are heirs of Rashi, Rambam and the Vilna Gaon, exemplars of the great rational heritage and the struggle to find meaning within the text of the Torah. Yet we are also descended from Shimon bar Yohai and Isaac Luria, kabbalists who taught us through their mystical teachings that God is everywhere. Proud of our heritage, we are not ashamed to remember the pain of our history as well. We bear the obligation to remember that Auschwitz and the pogroms are also our recent legacy. The works of the great secular Yiddish writers are as much a part of our consciousness as the contributions of modem day Israel to our sense of pride and national purpose. Our historical memory is seared into our consciousness and woven into the very fabric and essence of our being. Let its message inspire us.

One of the most profound thinkers in the American Jewish community today, Rabbi Harold Schulweis, has written in his book *For Those Who Can't Believe,* "(Most people) send their children to know about religion, not to believe; to know about ritual, not to observe; to know how to pray, not to pray; to know something about Jewish history, not to be engaged in the people's way of life. But knowing is not believing, knowing is not behaving, knowing is not belonging." I, too, believe that we must come together to learn about our heritage, but let us also come here to our synagogue to express our tradition and to strengthen it by living it.

As I have said previously one of the primary benefits of coming to synagogue is to hear what it is that God demands of us. Here in the synagogue we can, as a community, express our moral outrage at the complicity of the world in the shedding of innocent lives. Here we can condemn the carnage that is going on and see the parallels to the Jewish experience throughout the millennia and to understand the Jewish imperative to act. We come together as a synagogue to understand how the calling of our tradition, our prophets and sages applies to the realities of today.

Sometimes, what we are searching for and how to carry on the search seems unclear, but our common quest brings us together. The idea of coming together in our search reminds me of the Chelm story about the man who was looking for a purse that he lost. A friend offered to help and asked him where he lost it. He said he lost it in the field. "So if you lost your wallet in the field, then why are you looking over here by the barn?" the friend asked incredulously, to which the man replied, "Because over here the light is better."

Here in the synagogue we can search somewhat better, because we have more light when we search together in the company of others and in the light of our ancient and noble heritage. Here we find a community of seekers with whom we can share our joys and sorrows.

This past year I went to a *Grateful Dead* concert with my kids. I am not a fan of the *Grateful Dead,* but my son, Ezra, is. I went because he really wanted to see them in concert, and I wasn't too keen on him going by himself. Furthermore, I was curious and wanted to see first-hand what the phenomenon was all about. No sooner had we parked the car, when someone approached Micha, my 12 year old, and said to him, "Hey man, do you got any dope, or spare change so I can buy some?" And he said that with me accompanying my child! That was not my only surprise.

What is it about the *Grateful Dead* that aroused such an intense following? Groups of people follow the *Dead* from concert to concert and from city to city. Music was part of it, but having heard them, believe me, I knew it had to be more than just the music. I learned that the real attraction was the sense of sharing and community. The woman who was next to me at the concert told me that at one time she followed the group on a national tour mainly because she found acceptance for whom and what she was. Most of all, she said, she found a community. In our increasingly technological society many people seek to be part of a group.

We need to ensure that we create a sense of community and belonging here in our synagogue.

Describing the creation of a community, the promotional material for the new JCC in the District of Columbia proclaims, "We're not building a building. We're building a community." It is easier said than done, and it may even be easier to build a building than a community, but this is the challenge we face. Building a community is accomplished by the simple things we do for each other and with each other. It is created when we give of ourselves for a greater good. It comes from the fellowship of working with others in the kitchen on a Friday morning, of attending a Sunday morning minyan or shabbat service or by participating in any of the myriad of activities in which you can get involved.

Rabbi Arnold Jacob Wolf of Chicago recently wrote that one of the major mistakes made by rabbis today is that we do not make enough demands on our congregants. In urging rabbis to help educate their congregants to better understand the expectations of our heritage, he wrote, "Judaism is about demands, not about services. It's about what you give, not what you get."

We make the mistake of viewing our communal institutions as places where we can place demands upon those who are providing services, without realizing that

Judaism is what summons us. We assume that in America, since the customer is always right, the person who pays the bill can determine how things should be done. Too many people look upon synagogues as what has been called "service station Judaism." They pull in for a fill up, expecting the synagogue to be there to serve their needs for bar or bat mitzvah or religious school, without giving consideration to their obligation.

Let us think, not just in terms of what we expect to get out of synagogue, but in terms of what we can offer our community to strengthen it. Let us not think in terms of what the synagogue owes us or should do for us, but what we can do to help enhance the synagogue's efforts to perpetuate Judaism into the next century and beyond. We need you to get involved in social action projects, to take adult education classes, to attend services, to think together about the future of Judaism. And yes, we also need your financial support.

I referred earlier to the powerful imagery of the letters on the wall. In fact, the Talmud states that when any one letter of the Torah scroll is missing, the entire scroll is invalid; it takes all the letters to tell the story. From this we infer that for a community to be whole all members of the community need to be present.

The pattern on our wall happens to end with the letter *tzaddik,* the symbol of righteousness and humility, as in the word "tzedek", and B'nai Tzedek, meaning justice. Coincidence? Perhaps, or perhaps when we are in the sanctuary we should see a reminder of life's greater purpose and of our obligation to work for *tikun olam,* to repair the world by pursuing justice and righteousness.

I want to conclude with a beautiful story about Rebbe Menachem Mendel, who was teaching the students in his *bet midrash,* house of study, after the conclusion of their morning prayers. Word came to them that a man had ascended the Mount of Olives and had blown the shofar to announce the arrival of the Messiah. The rebbe tried to calm his students, and so he told his hasidim that he would step outside into the street to verify if the rumor was true. He came back and reported to his students that the Mashiach had not arrived.

His disciples were disappointed, but wanted to know how he could be so sure, so quickly. Furthermore, they asked why he had to go outside to ascertain whether or not the news was true. He told them, "When I stepped out into the village, I saw that people were still competitive and filled with contempt for each other. I saw that they had not changed in how they act towards each other, and so I realized that the Messiah still had not yet arrived. I had to go outside of our *bet midrash* to find out if the messiah had arrived because here in our place of study, there is always so much love and so much caring, it feels as if the Messiah is already here."

I pray that just as the rebbe had felt a bit of the messianic presence in his *shtiebel* that we, with your help and God's blessing, may also be able to bring a taste of the messianic era to our synagogue community as well. May we create a community in which we feel the harmony and the blessing of the Messianic Age. May we receive the blessing of a taste of the world to come through our efforts to create a special place, a place where the letters and words of Torah will lift us towards the heaven above.

Rosh Hashana
5756 / 1995

A Tale of Two Synagogues

I want to share a story with you this morning. To paraphrase Charles Dickens, it is a tale of two synagogues. It was the best of synagogues. It was the worst of synagogues.

One synagogue was warm and friendly with a sense of community. The members were receptive to newcomers and encouraged them to get involved. At the other synagogue, no one went out of his or her way to befriend people they did not know.

One synagogue was open to all, regardless of financial means. In fact, when a wealthy member asked for preferential treatment in the assigning of a bar mitzvah date, he learned that the process was blind and fair. The other synagogue was known to cater to the wealthy supporters.

One took care of people in time of need. Financial wherewithal was never an impediment to membership, for the generosity of its affluent members allowed it to accept even those who could not afford to pay full dues. At the other they always seemed to ask members for money.

One had a dynamic and creative religious school. The other placed numerous demands and requirements upon its students and their families.

Both rabbis were known for their creativity as well as their strong oratory and teaching skills. One rabbi was always there for people, was warm and welcoming, and went out of his way for all congregants. The rabbi of the other, as may be expected, was mainly interested in the wealthy and original members.

I probably should not go any further or tell you any more about the two synagogues, for fear that you may figure out whom I am discussing. I know both rabbis, and they would probably be upset if I told you any more details. But at the risk of going out on a limb and embarrassing a colleague, out of fairness I am going to reveal to whom I am referring.

The names of the two synagogues in this parable are B'nai Tzedek and B'nai Tzedek. That's right – your synagogue.

Most of you belong to the first one, while some of you may feel you belong to the second one. As is so often the case with everything in life, what you make of it and how you view things are what actually determine your reality.

I speak to you about our congregation on this holy day, because this day of national convocation offers us the unique opportunity to reflect upon both personal and communal concerns. As we are gathered here in this sacred place, our beloved home, we come together to reflect upon the meaning of our lives, to search for a connection to our tradition and to a Greater Being. In that context, also appropriate on this day, is reflecting upon our connection to our own community and considering our collective fate and future.

The synagogue is where we turn in times of trouble and need. It is the place where we educate our children and ourselves. It is the fountainhead of Jewish life where we come for inspiration and meaningfulness. The synagogue offers us the sense of community, continuity and comfort, as well as connectedness to our heritage, our ancestors, and our fellow Jews. It is the place where we come to pursue our quest for spirituality.

While my talk this morning is about the

synagogue, this discussion has to do with important teachings about Judaism and life itself. As the opening tale so poignantly demonstrates, the synagogue is what you make of it, what you project onto it. As I have said before, the judgments we make and the critical opinions we form often reveal more about the individual expressing the opinion than the object of the critique.

For example, you may know the story of the child who received a shiny new train set for his birthday and who took the gift in stride, showing little excitement or emotion. At the same time another child was taken to a barn where he was presented with a big pile of manure. He was ecstatic. His parents couldn't understand how he could be so happy, while the other child was so blasé about his gift. The second child explained, "With all this horse manure, I know there must be a pony in here somewhere." If nothing else, take that message with you – life is how you view things and what you make of it.

The New Year is a time for us to think about the personal and spiritual goals we each wish to establish and aspire to reach. As I mentioned on Rosh Hashana, the historic message of these Days of Awe pertains primarily to the work we need to do in terms of our own character flaws and repairing relationships. But in addition to our personal private petitions and concerns, note that the prayers we recite are in the plural to remind us to always be cognizant of the community and our role in it. A key element of the Yom Kippur liturgy reminds us not to be self-centered or absorbed in our own issues and lives, but to also reflect upon our obligations to the community. The balance between the two is part of the beauty of Judaism and one of the reasons, having addressed personal issues on Rosh Hashana, for the importance to consider this broader subject today.

Many of us are in the fortunate position of having the means and resources to participate in the sacred task of building a house of God, of continuing the ongoing process of making our facility fully functional. Expanding our facility is not a luxury but a necessity, so that we can better serve all of our current members and the vast array of creative and innovative programs we offer. Our building is not designed for three days, but for the vibrant congregation we are 365 days a year.

The kind of facility we will ultimately have will depend upon your response.

A story is told about a village where the rabbi asked people to each bring some wine for a special celebration to be enjoyed by the entire community. A funny thing happened. One fellow came and instead of pouring wine into the vat, poured water. He said to himself, "If I put in a little bit of water instead of pouring wine, it won't make much of a difference. After all, I am only one person." Another guy thought since everyone else is pouring in wine, it really is not so important what I give, so I will just pour water rather than wine. And so it went. When the time came for the big celebration, the spigot was turned and cups filled and passed around. Lo and behold, as you may have anticipated, to the embarrassment of all, what came out was 100% pure water. Everyone had assumed the other person was going to do the right thing and make the proper contribution, so no one did.

I hope that no one is upset because we speak today about the need to raise funds for the synagogue. I personally hate when I am trying to listen to an important story on National Public Radio only to feel as if I am being held hostage to one of their incessant fundraising campaigns.

Speaking of hostages, did you hear about the

terrorists who take over a synagogue and capture the rabbi, cantor and president? The terrorists ask the three for their last requests before torturing and killing them. The cantor says, "I have been practicing my recitation of the *Hineni* prayer. I would like to chant it one last time." The terrorist turns to the rabbi and asks what his last request is. He explains, "I have written a brilliant sermon for the High Holidays. I would like to give it before you execute me." Then he turns to the president of the shul and makes him the same offer. When he is asked, "What is your last wish?" He quickly responds, "Take me first."

I hope you don't feel that way.

I want you to understand that what I am trying to do is not so much help raise funds for our capital campaign, but to raise consciousness and to teach that how we spend our resources is something we should also ponder during the holy time of the *Yamim HaNoraim.* It is very much a focus and concern of Jewish sages throughout the ages. If you don't believe me, check out the words of what it is we ask of God more than anything else throughout these Ten Days of Awe. Our prayers ask that we be inscribed on these holy days in the Book of Life. The exact words are, *"b'sefer haim, berakha, v'shalom, ufarnasah tovah,* meaning: In the book of life, blessing, peace and parnasah *tovab,* a good living." *Parnasah,* livelihood – we ask for it explicitly on these days. In fact, of all that we pray for – life, blessing and peace – *parnasah is* the only one with an adjective attached to it, *tovah.* The rabbis explain that just making a living is not enough; it needs to be a good one. And what is a good living? They teach that *parnasah tovah* does not refer to how much we earn, but to how we spend what we earn. They further advise us to spend our *parnasah,* our income, *l'tovah* for good and worthy purposes. You can choose to spend lavishly on yourself or you can spend your resources for the betterment of others, *l'tovah.* The choice is yours.

The message of our tradition may not be very popular these days, but it is relatively simple. You are not entitled to remove yourself from the community. You are obligated to think about your responsibility to others. An inclusive project like this one, which offers the opportunity to make a lasting contribution and a significant difference in the community, does not come along too often in one's lifetime.

The other night one of our older members came up and told me how much she enjoyed being a part of all that we are doing. She said, "I know that the real thing you are most interested in is not just to build a beautiful building, but to build Jews." She was absolutely right.

Our goal is to bring people into our synagogue who previously had little connection to their Judaism. Our mission is to share our enthusiasm for the beauty of our heritage with those who have drifted away or who never did anything, as well as with those who serve as role models and who have deepened their level of observance and commitment as a result of their membership. Participation in a vibrant congregation is enriching. The recent Torah dedication ceremony was an inspiring and uplifting day for all, combining a love of our tradition with enthusiasm and an appreciation for the spiritual dimension in all that we do. We have succeeded in creating a dynamic community which seeks to grow in its commitment to living a meaningful Jewish life.

The synagogue, this synagogue in particular, has brought Judaism into the lives of so many as it seeks to reach out, teach and inspire and instill within our members a love for our tradition. I cannot begin to tell you how many people have told me that their affiliation has had a significant impact on their lives. Through exposure to our family education programs, retreats, adult education, and worship services, Judaism has come to play a larger role than before in the lives of an unbelievably large portion of our membership. If what we do has not yet touched you, if you haven't yet become a regular participant, let this be the year you start coming to services on a regular basis, the year that you learn Hebrew or take an adult education class.

It's really up to you as to which synagogue you choose to belong to. This is a truly magical place where spiritual journeys occur.

Or it can be a place where you can kvetch. I have been reading lately about research in the field of Jewish genetic diseases. One recent discovery has found a common gene among all *kohanim. I* would like to make my contribution to the field of Jewish genetic research. I have come to the conclusion that for some unknown reason, something inherent in our genes, makes us kvetch. I call it the "K" chromosome.

Kvetching probably had its origins in the very beginning of our formation as a people upon our departure from Egypt. Moses encountered it when he led the children of Israel out of slavery, and they kept longing for the days when they were well fed in Egypt. One of my favorite stories from the *midrash* is about Reuven and Shimon who walked through the Sea of Reeds. As the Egyptian army was in hot pursuit, God opened up the Sea, and a wall of water appeared on either side. The people marched through safely as God performed this most spectacular of miracles. But the whole time they were walking through the sea, these two guys, Reuven and Shimon, were complaining about the mud on the floor of the sea that was getting all over their sandals.

We are never satisfied, as in the story about a guy who goes into a restaurant. The maitre d' asks him how he enjoyed the meal. He said, "Not bad, but not enough bread – only two slices." The next day the guy returns to the restaurant, and again the maitre d' asks how he liked his lunch. This time the diner receives four slices of bread, but again complains that it isn't enough. The following day they see him coming and put out six slices, and again he isn't satisfied. Finally, the next day the owner tells the waiter – take the whole loaf, cut it in two and give it to him. Asked how he likes the meal this time, the guy says, "There you go again – back to two slices!"

I hope that everyone participates willingly in the capital campaign, because it is an opportunity to be a part of something bigger. Let me put it in terms that are especially meaningful. Rabbi Alexander Schindler captured the spirit, essence and significance of this institution and the relationship and interdependence among our homes, our community and the synagogue when he wrote:

"Our lives are a wilderness, uncharted and unpredictable – untimely deaths, unexpected blows, unfulfilled dreams. And yet, by gathering our heartaches into a house of worship, we find something transformative happening – our sorrows become windows of compassion. Paths through the wilderness, hewed and marked by past generations, give us our bearings. Patterns of meaning and significance merge. We are moved from self-pity to love. Our individual heartbeats merge with the pulse of all humankind. Suddenly, we no longer tremble like an uprooted reed."

We should always keep this in mind when we participate in efforts to build a shul. I think of the story about the shul where a man made a significant pledge of $250,000 to the building campaign. It took the synagogue years, much aggravation and even entailed costly litigation to get the money pledged. When they launched a second campaign a few years later, once again the same businessman was swept up and caught up with the passion of the rabbi's appeal. Again he made a generous pledge of $250,000. He looked around and recognized that all the moans and groans were coming from the previous leadership who remembered all they went through the first time. He then got up to amend his pledge and added to the relief of all, "$250,000, plus attorney's fees."

Morrie Schwartz, in *Tuesdays with Morrie,* by Mitch Albom, explains what it means to be a part of something greater than any one individual. He related the story of a wave that was having a great time bobbing up and down on the ocean. Suddenly the wave got upset because it realized it was about to crash into the sand of the seashore and that it would soon be annihilated, its life over. Another wave that came bobbing along consoled the first, asking, "Why are you so depressed?" The first wave said, "You don't understand. You're going to crash into that shore and soon you and I, we will all be nothing." To which the other wave responded, "No, it is you who does not understand. You are not just a wave. You are part of the ocean."

The way to find meaning and a sense of purpose in life is to link ourselves with something greater than ourselves, something of lasting eternal value. I think that is the inherent pull and attraction of these Days of Awe, the chance to be part of a wonderful people with a beautiful and rich heritage and the chance to renew our commitment to live by its historic principles. We almost never regret when we do a *mitzvah*. More often than not, however, we do regret later that which we do not do. I hope you will each join in this sacred and blessed task as we continue our work of building *a kehillah kedosha,* a holy congregation.

Yom Kippur
5759 / 1998

An Open Letter: Thinking About Dropping Out?

Dear Congregant,

I understand that, since your children are about to go off to college, you have decided not to renew your membership.

While I wish you a *mazel tov* and wish your family well, I must let you know how disappointed I am in your decision.

I recall celebrating with you, your family and friends at your daughter's bat mitzvah as well as at your son's bar mitzvah. The joy was heightened because a community shared these milestones in your family's life. Teachers and members of our staff played a vital role in making these events possible. Volunteers and congregants did their share behind the scenes to make sure everything was just right.

I recall consoling you at the time of the loss of your mother. But again I was not there alone. Members of the congregation came to the *Shiva,* both people you knew and people you did not know, in order to comfort you and help see you through a difficult time. That is what one Jew does for another, and this offer of help is what happens when you are part of a synagogue community.

By choosing to leave the congregation you are saying that you no longer wish to support the community that provided the environment, infrastructure and the extended family that helped to make these *simchas* possible and who offered comfort and strength in times of sorrow. Our caring committee was there to offer support during times of travail in a variety of ways. If you do not remain a member you would appear to be turning your back on the community, on the support structure and on all of these individuals. I am disappointed that you would consider not renewing your membership for we as a community were there for you at important times in your life.

Although you have chosen so far not to avail yourself of the many wonderful adult education programs we offer, they were also there for you. As I recall, you did participate in some of our social action programs dedicated to helping to fulfill our obligation as Jews to work for *tikun olam,* to make the world a better place. We were glad that you worked with us on the mitzvah of *tikun olam,* making the world a better place.

You might think that since you don't "use the Temple," continuing to pay for it doesn't make sense. Yet, even though you did not frequently attend services or participate in all that we offer, your being a member supported the congregation. Your financial support of the institution allowed others to belong, who might not have been able to afford it.

I have always maintained that the synagogue is on the front line in Jewish life. Our programs, classes and activities for adults, children and youth, reinforce and strengthen Jewish life in the home and community. Along with other communal institutions we play a crucial role in the survival of Judaism.

Synagogue membership should not be viewed the same way you view membership in a country club. Just because you may not come that often and may not think you make full use of its services and programs, does not mean you should leave the community.

I recently heard an author say that it is good to

buy a book even if you do not have time to read it. Even if it just sits on the bookshelf, having the volume is a means of aligning oneself with the thought and thrust of an author's work and of showing support for the author's ideas. We could say the same about being a member of a synagogue that you do not attend very often. Your affiliation means that you are supporting the local Jewish community. By so doing, you also send a message to your children about the importance of being a member of the community. Not being a member sends them a message as well.

So I urge you to reconsider your decision. Rather than viewing synagogue membership as a discretionary expense, I suggest that now may be an ideal time to involve yourself more, to take advantage of what we offer you. Precisely now when your children are older, you have more time to sample the classes, join a committee, attend services, come to Brotherhood and Sisterhood functions and partake in some of the many wonderful things which we offer. At the very least your membership is a tax-deductible contribution that goes towards the work of perpetuating Judaism and the Jewish people. Your dues help to support the vital educational programs we offer, the creative and dynamic social, cultural and religious services of B'nai Tzedek. And, finally, think of it as better than an insurance policy. Your membership ensures not just assisting the continuity of the Jewish people as a whole, but also that our staff, facility and infrastructure will always be here for you and others you know.

I sincerely hope you will reconsider your decision and continue to maintain your membership.

September 2005

The Joy of Being a Rabbi

This was unquestionably a tough year for business, especially for people in my line of work. It was a tough year for religion and for those who practice it.

The Catholic Church scandal, which has been brewing for years, exploded full force with the cumulative impact of the exposure of numerous cases of pedophilia by its clergy. No longer is it possible to ignore or view the large number of cases as aberrations. These crimes took a significant toll on countless individuals and caused irreparable damage, shattering many lives. It will be difficult for the church to reestablish its esteem since it bears responsibility for complicity and cover-up of the scandal.

One Catholic archbishop sought to explain the crisis by blaming it on – you guessed it: the Jews! Somehow, it always comes back to being about us. Cardinal Oscar Andres Rodriquez Meridiaga said that the story is old and that the only reason we are hearing about it now is that the Jewish media wanted to give these long-past incidents prominence and played them up in order to divert attention away from criticism of Israel. The scary thing is that this guy is not some marginal kook, but is actually pretty high up in the Church hierarchy and is mentioned as a possible successor to the Pope. How reassuring to hear his accusations – just when I was worried that our power and influence were on the decline!

On the local scene, *The Washington Post* has chronicled the situation of a minister who was discovered passing off the sermons of others as his own. It diminishes the level of trust worshippers place in the authenticity of their leader and his message.

And speaking of unearned or misplaced trust, in New Jersey a rabbi accused of murdering his wife eight years ago was convicted of the crime and sent to prison. Arthur Magida, author of the book, *The Rabbi and the Hit Man,* has been covering the story for a number of years. He was attracted to the story because of the theme of tension between the *yetzer hatov* and the opposing *yetzer hara,* the inclination to evil. He says, "I see that evil's great, fearsome talent is its power to creep up on us, bit by bit and day by day, until we say farewell to our better side, to our *yetzer hatov."* In a scathing indictment of the rabbi he writes, "He stole the souls of his congregants, the hearts of his children and the life of his wife. His very life is a sharp, scolding sermon: do not trespass, it says, where I have been, for I have met evil and I have done evil and I am evil."

Yes, it was a tough year for religion.

And then we heard from the Moslem clerics who sanction and express sympathy for acts of murder. It is beyond me why Sheik Ahmed Yassin, the mastermind behind the terrorist organization Hamas, is referred to as a "spiritual leader." Billy Graham is a spiritual leader. The chief rabbi of Israel is a spiritual leader. The Pope is a spiritual leader. The rabbi of Temple Emanuel of New York is a spiritual leader. Sheik Yassin is the head of a group of terrorist thugs, but he is not a spiritual leader.

With leaders and role models like these – a plagiarist, a philanderer, pedophiles, conspirators, murderers and terrorists – one can understand the cynicism towards religion and religious leaders among the population. It is of little consolation that religious leaders are not the only ones guilty of indiscretions and terrible errors in judgment.

Having been misled so often, people wonder if they can place their trust in politicians. In the realm of big business, executives of Tyco, Enron, and Worldcom have recently received prison sentences for their crimes and the lies they told about their company's finances. In the world of the print media *The New York Times* was embarrassed by the case of Jayson Blair, a bright, arrogant, rising star who fabricated stories and quotes. He should have learned from an earlier, similar incident at the *Washington Post*.

I am disturbed by what has transpired in the religious community, in part because this is my profession. Heinous acts of some religious leaders reflect on all members of the clergy and also reveal something about our greater society. Furthermore, the *Yamim HaNoraim* lend themselves to the theme of introspection and reflection. We set aside this time to think of what we may be guilty and how we want to grow and change in the coming year. Perhaps I am musing about the implications of these matters because this coming spring will mark the 25th anniversary since I became an ordained rabbi.

I am thinking about personal issues for this is not the only life cycle event on my mind these days. This past year I celebrated the milestone of my 50th birthday. And just last month we celebrated with joy the bar mitzvah of my youngest son, Noam.

Finally, I find myself in a particularly pensive and reflective mood because the past few weeks have also been somewhat emotionally wrenching and draining. My family has been in the process of dismantling the home in which I grew up, since my father just this week moved out of his home of over 46 years and into an assisted living home. The walls are bare. The house is stripped of the furniture. The *tzochtzhes,* each with their own memories and associations, and all the things that made it a home are gone. The building is a shell and is on the market for sale.

Such are the cycles of life.

Stephen Fried, author of *The New Rabbi,* writes about the convergence of events. "Changing lives is the theme of the entire High Holiday season. Rosh Hashana is a celebration of the new year and its possibilities; it signals the beginning of a period of taking emotional, personal and theological inventory."

In the spirit of reflection I think of earlier years and recall my decision to become a rabbi and to devote my life to serving God and the Jewish people. It was not until late in my senior year of college that I chose to apply to rabbinical school.

While my Christian colleagues speak of receiving the "call" to become a minister, we Jews usually do not speak in such terms. For me it was most definitely not a calling from beyond, but much more a voice from within. Ultimately, the survival of the Jewish people and of Judaism is the most important thing in the world to me. This conviction, coupled with my desire to use whatever God-given talents I possess to serve God and His people, made the choice a logical one.

My first experience as a rabbi came when I was a student in rabbinical school. After a year of *ulpan* in Israel, where I learned to conjugate verbs and the difference between the *hifil* and *niphal* forms, the rabbinical program thrust me upon the unsuspecting Jewish families of Harlingen, Texas for my first High Holiday leadership experience. I was apprehensive, knowing that people would be looking to me as their rabbi. I just kept worrying what I would do if they asked me about anything other than Hebrew grammar, since that was about all I knew after a year of Hebrew studies in rabbinical school in Jerusalem. Somehow I survived, and so did they.

The next year, now a veteran of introductory courses in *midrash,* Bible and Talmud, I once again took on a high holiday pulpit. When I asked my bride, new to America, where she would like to go, she said somewhat adventurously, "Choose the farthest congregation available." So we wound up in Caspar, Wyoming, where I returned for the next three years.

The reasons I decided to become a rabbi are as compelling for me today, as they were when I first started thinking about becoming a rabbi almost 30 years ago. The survival of Judaism and the Jewish people still motivates me. Study of Jewish sources and Jewish texts continues to excite me. I find so many wonderful messages and meaning in them. I delight in the way in which such ancient writings seem so contemporary and have such profound applications and relevance for today. I revel in the challenge of finding the best ways to share its message with you and struggle with how to convey and impart my passion, convictions and enthusiasm to you. Needless to say, I still have a deep love of the Jewish people, continue to worry about our survival, and agonize over our future.

In many respects the issues confronting the Jewish communities and congregations I have been blessed to serve remain the same. I enjoy the challenge of imparting a love of Judaism to our members, of helping them to realize that without rituals and customs our heritage cannot be passed on to the next generation; of teaching those traditions; of helping people realize that Judaism is more than just a set of vague ideas, concepts and values. Our faith is spiritually rewarding when lived in the context of home and community, and can profoundly affect how we conduct our daily lives. I enjoy helping congregants feel connected and part of a people. I am moved by the potency of the intellectual sophistication of our texts and appreciate the beauty of celebrating the holidays, Shabbat, and life cycle events. It is gratifying to see how meaningful, especially at times of loss and death of a loved one, fully observing the *halakha* and *minhagim* customs can be and how helpful they are to people going through a difficult time. I am pleased to witness our members be inspired and uplifted by the majesty of our liturgy, as well as to feel both the pain of our people's suffering and the joy of our celebrations. To be a Jew is to appreciate our accomplishments and sense of humor and to celebrate our unique outlook and perspective on life.

The converse is also true, for the absence of Judaism can lead to unfortunate circumstances. A number of years ago a congregant spoke with me about the concerns he had, as his 15-year old teenage daughter, like many of her friends, was spending Friday nights going to parties and getting drunk. What can we expect when we do not offer and strongly encourage our children to accept the anchor that is presented by our tradition. Just think how, in this instance, celebrating Shabbat at home would have provided a framework that could have helped prevent this situation.

And to illustrate my point about how relevant Judaism is to our lives, the Talmud tells the story of a child who is overly sheltered and protected, whose every need is met by overindulgent parents. The father places a pouch of gold around the child's neck and sends him to stand outside a house of ill repute. The Talmud asks, "Does he really expect that his son will not sin?!" The story beckons to us from across the ages and warns us of the consequences of giving our children everything, without placing any limits or restrictions on them. It calls upon us to come to terms with our responsibility for the consequences of the choices we make and to take steps to prevent the inevitable outcome caused by our shortsightedness.

In biblical times our ancestors contended with idolatry. The rabbis of the Talmud as in our day already knew that the idolatry of their times was materialism. Over-loading ourselves with objects speaks to the vacuity we feel, due to the paucity and emptiness of our values. Deep down when we are honest with ourselves, as we must be on this day, we agonize over the bankruptcy, hollowness and shallowness of our lives when we realize how much time and energy is expended pursuing pleasure and bigger and more material things. These are among the most serious problems facing all of us.

I have yet to meet a parent who says they want their children to be materialistic. Every Jew I know says they want their children to have values. They say family is the most important thing to them. How do we propose to instill values if we ourselves are not familiar with and conversant in them? How can we pass them on if we do not put the ideals of our faith into practice? And in reality, merely emphasizing family or family togetherness can be only self-serving if it is an end in itself. What is the antidote to a materialistic, narcissistic society? How do we learn to say no to our children and to ourselves and to set limits? What do we have to do in order to achieve a balance in our lives? How do we learn that happiness comes not just from what we have, but from a combination of what we are, how we act and treat others, and how we feel about ourselves? These are the questions we must grapple with, and in every instance I remain convinced the answer is Judaism.

Being a rabbi is an exciting and challenging undertaking, offering the opportunity to touch people, to address the issues confronting us, to teach and thereby make a difference in people's lives not only in our community but in our wider world. Just the other day I received a call from the head of the campaign of one of the leading candidates for the Democratic nomination for President. The call was in response to concerns I expressed in a letter about recent statements the candidate had made about the Middle East. The conversation ended with the request that I send along any suggestions I had for language the candidate should include in upcoming speeches about Israel. A few days before Rosh Hashana I spoke at a rally in front of the Embassy of Saudi Arabia protesting their support of Hamas and fundamentalist Islamic terrorists. This was my third speech in front of an Arab embassy in recent months, as I had served as the keynote speaker at rallies in front of the Egyptian and Syrian embassies as well.

As energizing and fulfilling as the public policy role may be, I also value the quiet private moments of counseling or consoling a couple, of offering support to a congregant in a difficult or trying time like joblessness, or speaking with a child about what is bothering him or her. Knowing that even people in need of a job can feel comfortable confiding in me can be deeply rewarding.

One of my favorite aspects of this blessed work is the opportunity to share special moments in the lives of congregants and their families. I will never forget the first time I officiated at a funeral as a student rabbi in Muncie, Indiana. Only a handful of people, all members of the congregation, were in attendance, as the only surviving relative was his non-Jewish wife. She insisted that before the funeral I take a look and see how nicely she had him made up, with his glasses on his eyes (as if this is going to help him see better, I remember thinking to myself). At the conclusion of the service imagine my surprise when the funeral director proceeded to the front of the chapel and announced to the assembled guests, "I just want everyone here to know that this is this young man's very first funeral. And I am sure you will all agree with me that he did an outstanding job." Somewhat sheepishly I accepted the congratulations of the people there and tried to leave before they started to applaud and give me a standing ovation.

My next funeral, this time my first as an ordained rabbi, was in Miami, Florida. A meeting with the children of the deceased yielded little information about the man I was supposed to eulogize. So just before the service I met the gentleman's attorney. In order to elicit some more information I said to him, "Abe must have been quite *a* guy." He responded, "Rabbi, you are one of the lucky ones. You didn't know him."

While I find it extremely stimulating, challenging and fulfilling to serve the Jewish people, Dr. Jack Wertheimer, provost of the Jewish Theological Seminary, wrote this past May in *Commentary* magazine about the crisis of the diminished status of the American rabbinate today. He lamented the reduced role and authority of the rabbi in American Jewish life, saying we as a people are not better off under these circumstances. He said that, "The relevant question becomes not how much the rabbi knows about Judaism and how effectively he instills it, but how the rabbi treated me and my family at our life cycle event. . .and whether at our last encounter the rabbi uttered the words I needed to hear."

What is it that congregants really want? As Rabbi Elliott Schoenberg, director of placement for the Rabbinical Assembly, sums it up, congregations want as their rabbi someone who attends every meeting and is at his desk working until midnight, someone who is 28-years old, but with 30 years of experience, someone who relates well to teenagers, but spends all his time working with senior citizens, who is always available in his office, but is active in the community and constantly visiting congregants. A rabbi should be an effective leader, but let lay persons run the congregation, a person of principle yet flexible, firm in convictions, but with the wisdom not to impose them – basically, someone who does everything, but knows how to delegate, and will stay with the congregation forever, but not too long.

A synagogue hired a rabbi based on the glowing recommendation given by the president of his previous shul, who praised the rabbi saying he was like Moses, Shakespeare and God. After a few months the new shul realized that they did not quite get what they had expected. Their rabbi barely knew anything about Judaism, was extremely inarticulate, and did not get along with anyone. Angered, they called the person who gave such a positive reference and demanded an explanation. The president of the old shul said, "Everything I said is true. Like Moses he stammers and is a poor public speaker. Like Shakespeare he knows nothing of Judaism. And like God he has no human qualities."

Being a rabbi is especially rewarding when teaching a class or getting someone excited about taking on more *mitzvoth* and living a life of greater commitment to Judaism. But if asked to choose just one moment that is my favorite, I would have to say it is during the wedding ceremony when I am standing at the *chuppah.* The first to enter, I watch the drama unfold before my very eyes. From my vantage point I see the parents and sense all the emotions they feel and watch the groom standing awkwardly, anxiously awaiting his bride. How fortunate I feel to be a part of this transitional moment, to glimpse the future from the best seat in the house. As I watch the unfolding of this scene I often quietly say a blessing to myself, one I first heard uttered by Rabbi Samuel Karf shortly after my ordination. "*Baruch atah adonai,* blessed are you O Lord, king of the Universe, *she'asah lee rav 1'amo yisrael,* who has made me a rabbi to his people, Israel."

During other transitions I think of what Judith Viorst wrote in her book, *Necessary Losses:* "At each stage of our life we are going to be confronted with experiences that will require us to say goodbye; that will require us to relinquish something we may not want to relinquish; that will require us to move on whether we are ready for it or not. And yet if we can do that without denying it, fighting it, refusing it, we grow."

Indeed, time marches on and so must we. Yom Kippur is the part of the annual cycle during which we can say goodbye to those things we need to relinquish. That is part of the message of this season. Our tradition forces us at this time of year both to confront our past and to imagine our future.

Yom Kippur is the time when each of us can and should pause and think about what we have done this past year and what we hope to change about our actions and behaviors in the coming year. The observance of Yom Kippur affirms that we are constantly re-writing both our past and our future. On this day we must honestly face where we are personally and where we wish to go. To do that, we must truthfully deal with our past and who we are.

A colleague told me a story about a family that was proud of their ancestors who had come to America on the Mayflower and who decided to commission a family history. In the course of doing research the historian they hired found that the family tree included many prominent individuals, but he also discovered a great uncle who was executed in the electric chair. The historian assured the family that this revelation would not be a problem. He wrote in the book, "Uncle George occupied a chair of applied electronics at an important government institution, was attached to his position by the strongest of ties, and his death came as a real shock."

Yom Kippur is not a day for deception. We must be honest with ourselves to become what we should strive to be. Where we see faults, shortcomings, and practices we should not continue, we can identify what we need to change.

About this process, I quote again from Stephen Fried's marvelous and insightful book: "Yom Kippur, a day of atonement, solemn fasting, introspection and immersion in past misdeeds, is when the book is closed for the year. It is the April 15th of Judaism. And, like a tax day for the soul, it is spent doing last-second calculations of self-worth, all without the benefit of food or water."

At this solemn hour may each of us reflect on the meaning of this day. As the medieval Jewish philosopher, Bachya ibn Pakuda, wrote, "Days are like scrolls. Write on them that which you wish to have remembered." May we use our days wisely, and may we write on the scrolls deeds of loving kindness, of devotion to our loved ones, and of dedication to the principles of our religion, so that we will be inscribed in the Book of Life for a good year.

As we proclaim in the morning blessings: *Baruch atah adonai, eloheinu melech haolam,* Blessed are you, O Lord, our God, King of the Universe, *she'asani yisrael,* who has made me a Jew. I thank God for having made me a Jew, and I thank you for the opportunity to serve the Jewish people. May each of us in our own way serve God and His people in the coming year.

Kol Nidre
5764 / 2003